ABOUT COMPUTERS

Craig Fields

Harvard University

WINTHROP PUBLISHERS, INC., Cambridge, Massachusetts

LIBRARY OF CONGRESS CATALOGING IN PUBLICATION DATA

Fields, Craig, 1946–
    About Computers.

    Bibliography: p.
    1. Computers. I. Title.
QA76.F47   001.6'4   72-6952
ISBN 0-87626-004-0

Copyright © 1973 by Winthrop Publishers, Inc.
    17 Dunster Street, Cambridge, Massachusetts 02138

CONTENTS

8

OF WHAT USE ARE DIFFERENT KINDS OF COMPUTERS?

INTRODUCTION

This is a book for people who want to learn some basic facts about computers and have absolutely no background in the field. In order to read and understand this book it is not necessary to know anything about computers, mathematics, electronics, or science in general.

If we look at the books currently available about computers, we find that although each has its place, most of them do not provide basic, general, understandable information. One class of books may be termed "children's books." These books are not necessarily aimed at children, but they may as well be: their contents are superficial and spotty, and, most importantly, they make frequent reference to *magic* although computers are not, in fact, at all magical.

A second type of book contains many examples of how computers can be used. Such a book may be restricted to one particular field, such as business, or it may be more catholic in its taste. Nevertheless, it is very hard for the average reader to apply these individual examples to his own particular problems.

Many books are concerned with the electronics and mathematics of computers. Such books are generally aimed at experts and have definite prerequisites. More insidious are those books that are aimed at the layman. After reading an "elementary" book on the mathematics or electronics of computers, one is not yet prepared to really understand either the mathematics or the electronics, nor does one have a sense of what a computer really is.

Other books are concerned with particular computers. With that limited goal, they may be excellent. Nevertheless, computers do differ, although there are underlying principles that relate to almost all electronic computers currently in use. Such common principles are generally not elucidated in a book about a particular manufacturer's product because the goal of such a book is to provide someone with a working familiarity with a particular product.

Other popular texts deal with so-called problem-oriented computer languages, such as FORTRAN, PL-1, and so on. These books allow the novice, in a short time, to gain a working knowledge of computers in order to solve a certain type of problem. However, the user will never understand, from this approach, what computers really are and how they work. He will never be able to use the language as efficiently as he might and will always feel that computers are surrounded by mystery.

This book does not teach any computer electronics, any computer language, or the details of how to use any currently existing computer. In fact, when the reader is finished he will not be able to do anything with any computer in the world. However, the reader of this book should gain confidence and direction. He should be able to decide whether any of his everyday problems can be solved or helped through the use of computers. If they can, he should be able to decide what sort of computer to use. He can then proceed to learn how to use that computer by getting appropriate computer manuals, reading them, and trying to write programs (this is explained later in the book). Most importantly, this book should de-mystify the process of computer usage.

The reader should be able to switch from computer to computer as his requirements change. He should be able to solve his problems while having complete confidence that he has a reasonable understanding of what the computer is doing at all times. To this end, he should be able to use the computer with some efficiency.

The machines we are used to dealing with differ from computers in that we must direct their sequence of actions while they are in operation. Like other machines, computers have a limited number of things that they can do. However, we can decide on the order in which these things are to be done independently of their accomplishment. For example, let us assume that a greatly simplified automobile could do the following things: start, stop, speed up, slow down, turn right, and turn left. If these operations were controlled by six buttons in the automobile, we could, by pressing the buttons in the proper sequence and at the proper time, direct the automobile along a rather complex path. We do very much the same thing when we drive a normal automobile, except that the controls are not so simple. If such an automobile were to be made into a simple computer, it would need additional capabilities. It would be necessary for us to be able to specify the sequence of the operations we wished the automobile to follow, and the automobile would need additional apparatus for reading our sequence of instructions. We might specify the sequence of operations by writing them on a piece of paper. In this case, it would be necessary for the automobile to have a mechanical-optical mechanism for reading our handwriting on the paper and directing the parts of the automobile (steering apparatus, accelerator, brakes) to do the tasks, in order, that we specified. This proposed modification of a simplified automobile into a computer involves the coordination of a storage medium for our instructions (in this case, paper), and a mechanism for reading the instructions in our storage medium and directing the automobile on its path. Chapter 1 discusses what makes the computer different from other machines.

A computer differs from other machines in that it has a storage medium for a set of instructions (properly called the *memory*), and a mechanism for reading our instructions from the storage medium and carrying them out (a *central processing unit*). A memory and a central processing unit are central to the concept of a computer and they are discussed in greater detail in chapter 2.

Information has to flow from place to place within any computer. For example, in our modified automobile, information has to flow from our storage medium (instructions on paper) to the mechanism that reads the paper (an analog of a central processing unit). Similarly, control information has to flow from the paper-reading mechanism to the wheels, brakes, accelerator, etc. The information flow in a computer is discussed in chapter 3.

A computer that could not interact with the "outside world" would not be particularly useful. It is necessary for it to interact with the real world, and it does so via *peripheral* machines. For example, a typewriter is a typical peripheral machine. If a typewriter is properly connected to a computer system, we can type messages to the computer and the computer can type messages to us. This puts the computer on our own terms, so to speak. We are used to dealing with typed messages—we are not used to dealing with electrical impulses that are native to modern computers. The subject of such interactions is considered in chapter 4.

We tell computers what we want them to do by giving them a list of instructions to follow. The details of how to prepare instructions are discussed in various places in the book. The main point of chapter 5 is that we cannot give computers just any instruction that we can conceive of. Each computer can follow only a small number of instructions. To take a typical example, an individual computer may be able to do, at one time, any one of 100 things. We can give it a sequence of 5 or 10,000 things to do, but each one must be drawn from the computer's set of 100. Clearly, if we arrange the list in the proper order, we can get it to do a complicated job. In a sense, there is a real parallel between the computer's instruction set and our language. Each of us uses what is effectively a finite set of words, but by arranging these in the right order, we can make an amazing variety of statements.

Fortunately, there are a number of techniques that one can use in order to help gain the greatest benefit from a computer. The computer manufacturer obviously has a vested interest in seeing that people use his products and do so relatively satisfactorily. Hence, he can be of assistance in this job, and chapter 6 tells precisely how.

Not everyone can afford to own his own computer. If a computer is shared with others, some rules have to be set up so that users do not interfere with each other. There are two basic schemes commonly in use whereby computers can be shared among a number of users. One is called *time-sharing* and the other is called *batch*. These systems are described in chapter 7.

There are lots of problems suitable for computers, and there are lots of computers with varying capabilities. It is important for a person to match his particular problem to the most appropriate computer. Guidelines for doing this are given in chapter 8.

This book is short enough to be read in an evening or two. Perhaps, however, one should read it at a slower pace in order to absorb the material, for a lot is said in a few pages.

This book can be used for part of a college or high-school course. It has been used in a course attended by several dozen undergraduates. They came to understand the material, more or less, within two weeks, and then went on to spend another two weeks learning to use a specific computer. After this time they had gained sufficient proficiency and confidence to independently and quickly solve a number of interesting problems.

1

WHAT ARE COMPUTERS AND WHAT CAN THEY DO?

One of the things that makes it difficult to understand modern electronic digital computers is the fact that they are electronic. It is much easier to understand how a mechanical system works because we can see the parts move and interact. Because the workings of electronic machines are mostly hidden from the eye, we cannot easily discern their operation and so we tend to think of them as being mysterious. Therefore, rather than begin our discussion with electronic digital computers, we shall consider a mechanical computer with which we are all familiar—the player piano.

A conventional piano is a complicated mechanism for producing sounds. The sounds that are produced are all determined by how we strike the keys—the order in which we strike them, and how many we strike at one time. The ordinary piano does not have any notion of what has happened in the past or what will happen in the future. It sits before us awaiting our orders, and does each thing we ask as we ask it. A player piano, however, does have a capability for "remembering" what has happened in the past and for "seeing" what will hap-

1

pen in the future. The mechanism that gives the player piano these extra capabilities is comparable to the "memory" of a computer. The use of the term "memory" may be unfortunate, for a player piano cannot recall experiences or forget, as can a human memory. In the simplest case the player piano's memory consists of a long roll of paper into which holes have been punched. The holes in the paper are read by a mechanical or electromechanical contraption that causes the appropriate keys to be depressed. (See Figure 1-1.)

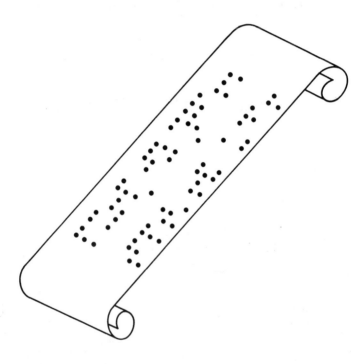

FIGURE 1-1. *The holes punched in rows across player piano paper are instructions; they tell the piano what to do.*

We could prepare a tune for the player piano by taking a roll of paper and punching holes in the right places. We could punch one or more holes in rows across the paper, thus indicating that one or more keys were to be depressed simultaneously. In addition, there would be a large number of rows, and the number of rows of holes would determine how long the composition was to be. We could then insert the paper into the player piano, position the beginning of our set of holes over the mechanism that reads the holes, and start the player piano. At this point, the roll would move continuously, and music would be produced. In a sense, each row of holes can be considered an instruction to the player piano. We decide on the sequencing of instructions to the player piano in advance, place them in the memory of the player piano (the roll of paper), start the paper at the beginning of our list of instructions, and then the player piano takes over the rest of the job. It interprets, sequentially, each instruction that we have punched into the paper, and without further human intervention it plays through to the end of the composition.

What will happen when the player piano reaches the end of the tune? It will continue to roll the paper but will find no holes. In that case, no more music would be produced and eventually the paper would come flopping off the bottom roll, or the top, as the case may be. In order to avoid this esthetically unpleasant situation, one could improve the basic mechanism of the player piano. For example, it might be possible to cut a notch into the paper in the extreme left-hand margin, so that whenever the player piano "sensed" a notch in that margin, it would automatically halt its rotation of the paper. More interesting player pianos could also be constructed so that a notch in the right-hand margin would indicate that the roll of paper should reverse direction. Such a player piano could play tunes both forwards and backwards. It would be easily possible to make player pianos more complicated than they usually are and to have them do more complicated things.

Let's briefly discuss what steps you would have to take in order to make a player piano play music you have composed. First, of course, you would do the creative work of thinking of a tune. Then you would write down this tune any way that you wished; for example, you could use conventional musical notation. Next, you would translate the conventional musical notation into a set of holes properly placed on the player piano roll; that is, you would have to decide where holes should be, and you would actually punch the holes in the paper. You could then take the roll of paper and place it in the player piano, positioning the beginning of your tune near the mechanism that will read it. Finally, you would start the player piano, which would read each of your instructions and press the keys to produce your tune.

Electronic digital computers are just like player pianos in many ways. They contain a storage medium into which you can write instructions. The instructions form a list, just like the list of instructions we have described for a player piano. After

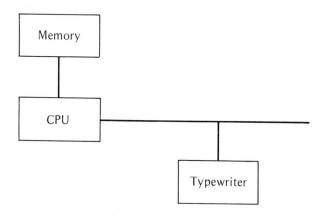

FIGURE 1-2. *A typical computer consists of a memory, a central processing unit, and a typewriter. The memory contains a list of instructions and the central processing unit takes each instruction from the list, in turn, and does whatever it indicates. For example, a list of instructions might cause the central processing unit to direct the typewriter to type a message.*

deciding on the list of instructions you want the computer to obey (or "execute") you would enter these instructions into the memory of the computer. Then you would position the computer to begin executing your instructions at the beginning of your list. You would start the computer, and at this point, it would examine (or "fetch") each instruction successively, and execute it. It would continue to do so until it fetched the instruction that tells it to halt—the so-called "halt" instruction.

Each instruction to a player piano indicates a particular combination of keys to be depressed. Thus, a complicated composition can be made up of a list of relatively simple instructions. Similarly, complex jobs can be done by computers by having them interpret lists of instructions, each instruction of which would be rather simple. Devices such as typewriters are connected to computers and individual instructions control the activity of the typewriter. Other kinds of instructions could do arithmetic calculations, or control simple machines such as tape recorders.

Many different media are used for the memories of electronic computers. In some cases, magnetic tape, similar to the magnetic tape used in home high-fidelity systems, is used. The instructions can be coded onto the magnetic tape rather than being punched into strips of paper as for the player piano. We could, for example, magnetize or demagnetize selected positions in rows across the tape, and an electronic mechanism could read the magnetized points to determine what instruction we want the computer to execute. In fact, the memories of computers are generally not based on magnetic tape, although they do make use of magnetism.

The section of the computer that fetches instructions and executes them is generally known as a *central processing unit*, or CPU. The CPU is comparable to that part of a player piano that reads the holes in the roll of paper and presses the appropriate keys. Central processors are electronic devices, and we will not discuss how they work in any great detail. A general computer system also includes machines that do something directly useful. In the case of the player piano the machine consists of keys, hammers, and wires that produce sounds. In the case of normal digital computers, the machines might consist of printers, typewriters, and other devices to interact with people. Without the central processor and the memory these devices would be comparable to an ordinary piano or typewriter. They would do exactly what you wish when you ask them to do something, but they would not be able to store a set of instructions and execute them.

There are serious limitations on the capability of a typical player piano. One limitation involves the kind of instructions that we can give to the player piano by punching holes in the paper tape. At a simple level, of course, we communicate what keys are to be depressed at what times. Anyone who has ever played the piano, however, knows that there are different ways to depress a key, and you can get different sounds from depressing the same key. With the simple player piano scheme I have outlined, there is no provision for pressing keys in different ways. However, one can conceive of a player piano in which holes are punched in the paper to indicate how a key is to be depressed. Such a player piano would be more versatile than an elementary one in that it would have a repertoire of more powerful instructions.

5

A player piano has a finite set of instructions, which we may call an *instruction set*. Similarly, a computer has its own instruction set. Each instruction causes the computer to do a small, finite task. We order these instructions into a list, and the computer executes the instructions one after the other until it interprets a "halt" instruction. The instruction set of a computer is determined by its electronic structure, which is designed and constructed by the manufacturer. Instruction sets differ from one computer model to another. You can find the instruction set of your computer by reading the manuals that are supplied by the manufacturer of the particular machine. The instruction set in any specific computer is designed by one or more persons, and the rules they use for deciding on what instructions to include and what instructions to exclude are usually poorly defined. Thus any instruction set is defined with a degree of arbitrariness, and the user of a computer simply accepts its instruction set as a constraint (and an aid) in solving his problems.

Just as there might be more or less powerful instruction sets for player pianos, there are more or less powerful instruction sets for computers. Some computers have individual instructions that can do a relatively complicated calculation; others require many instructions to do the same computation. For example, some computers have a single instruction that can be used to multiply two numbers. For other computers, where such an instruction is lacking, in order to multiply two numbers it would be necessary to add one number to itself over and over again. Hence, the more powerful the instruction set, the easier it may be to specify difficult tasks. One would think that all computers should be constructed with powerful instruction sets. Unfortunately, computers with powerful instruction sets have many more electronic parts and require more complex designs than their simpler counterparts. Therefore, computers with powerful instruction sets are usually considerably larger and more expensive than their simpler cousins.

Now let us consider the steps that one must follow in order to make a computer do something. The procedure is remarkably similar to the procedure for a player piano. The kind of problem appropriate for a player piano involves playing a particular tune. The kind of problem appropriate for computers involves a sequence of steps of calculation. First one would have to conceive of how to get the solution to a problem. This solution could be written down in any notation that proved comfortable to the user. Then the steps to be taken to achieve that solution would have to be written in terms that the computer could interpret, that is, in terms of the instruction set of the computer. The list of instructions would have to be entered into the memory of the computer, just as holes have to be punched into player piano paper. The computer could be told where the program is located in its memory, and where to start. This is similar to the positioning of the paper in the player piano. Finally, the computer could be started. At this point the central processor of the computer would sequentially fetch instructions and execute them until it reached a "halt" instruction.

If the user of a computer has to conceive of the solution to a problem, of what possible use is the computer? We may divide the process of problem solving into two parts: first, it is necessary to decide on the steps to be taken in order to reach the solution to a problem; second, it is necessary to actually do those steps. For some problems the first part is trivial, and the second part is long and tedious. For other problems, deciding on what to do is the hardest part of the task. Computers can help with the second stage of problem solving, for they can do the things we require, step by step, in order to achieve the solution to a problem.

I have invented two hypothetical computers and we will examine how they might operate. The first is called Drawing Computer 1, or DC-1 (Figure 1-3). If you purchased a DC-1, it would consist of a cabinet filled with electronics, and it would have some wires attached to it. These wires would be connected to a mechanical arm, and at the end of the mechanical arm would be a pen. You could position this pen over a piece of paper and then plug in the computer. Most computers have switches and lights on the front, and almost all computers have a switch that is labeled "start," or "begin." If, at this time, you press the switch labeled "start," and if the computer is not broken, it is very likely that absolutely nothing would happen. This is not surprising, because you have not yet written a program (a list of instructions) for the computer, and have not entered any instructions into the memory. Before you can use the DC-1 to solve any of your problems, you have to know what the instruction set is so that you can formulate your programs in terms of that particular instruction set.

Since I have made up DC-1, I can also make up an instruction set. This computer has only four instructions. The first instruction is "lift pen," abbreviated "LP"; the second is "drop pen," abbreviated "DP"; the third is "halt," abbreviated "HLT"; and the fourth is "go to x,y," abbreviated "GT x,y."

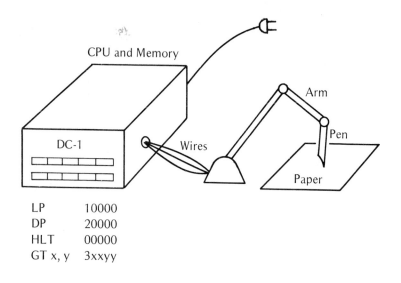

LP	10000
DP	20000
HLT	00000
GT x, y	3xxyy

FIGURE 1-3. *DC-1 is a hypothetical computer that has one peripheral device—an arm and pen for drawing pictures. Its instruction set is limited to four possible instructions: "lift pen," "drop pen," "halt," and "go to location x, y." Each instruction is represented by an appropriate number.*

The purpose of each of the first three instructions is fairly obvious. If the CPU of DC-1 fetched a "lift pen" instruction from a list of instructions it was executing, it would lift the pen from the paper or, if the pen were already lifted, would keep it in the air. The fourth instruction would cause the pen to move from wherever it was located to a point with Cartesian coordinates x,y. That is, to a point x units (inches, for example) to the right of the left hand side of the page and y units above the bottom of the page. For example, "go to 10,20" will cause the pen to move directly to the point 10,20, and so on. The "go to" instruction allows you to draw lines as short as you wish so that you can draw dots or curves composed of many short lines.

We have to find some way of entering our program into the computer, and we cannot do this by putting such letters as "l i f t   p e n," into the machine in any way. The memories of most computers cannot store letters directly, but they can store numbers, so each instruction must be translated into numbers, and the numbers can be entered into the memory of the computer. I shall tell you the arbitrarily chosen numbers associated with each of these arbitrarily chosen instructions. In a real computer, the numbers associated with each instruction are defined by the manufacturer. The "lift pen" instruction is coded as 10000, the "drop pen" instruction as 20000, the "halt" instruction as 00000, and the "go to x,y" instruction as 3xxyy. The xxyy here represents the coordinate numbers; for example, "go to 20,40" would be coded as 32040. Similarly, "go to 0,0" would be coded as 30000. You can't go to any point that has either x or y coordinates larger than 99. This is a limitation of this particular machine, and all machines have similar limitations.

With the instruction set, you can instantly produce a workable program for DC-1, such as the program to draw a square that is shown in Figure 1-4. The first instruction causes the pen to be lifted. The second causes it to go to location 0,0. (We lift the pen before going to 0,0 so that a line is not inadvert-

LP	10000
GT 0,0	30000
DP	20000
GT 50,0	35000
GT 50,50	35050
GT 0,50	30050
GT 0,0	30000
LP	10000
HLT	00000

FIGURE 1-4. *The left-hand column above shows the abbreviations for a list of instructions to draw a square. The middle column shows the numbers associated with each instruction. To the right we see the effect of the execution of each instruction.*

ently drawn on the paper.) We drop the pen and go to 50,0, thereby drawing the bottom side of the square. We then go to 50,50, thus drawing the right-hand side of the square. We go to 0,50 and to 0,0 to complete the square. At this point we lift the pen so that ink does not continue to flow out of it and create a messy drawing, and finally we halt. Each of the instructions can easily be translated into numbers using the rules that were described for DC-1; the list of numbers is indicated in Figure 1-4. It is now possible to put these numbers, in a list, into the memory of the computer, and to start the central processor fetching instructions from the beginning of that list. Instructions will continue to be fetched until the entire square is drawn, and then the computer will halt.

DC-1 is not a particularly interesting computer. It is so much trouble to use that it is probably easier to draw things with a ruler. The problem is that it has a limited instruction set.

I have "invented" a more interesting computer called Drawing Computer 2, or DC-2. DC-2 differs from DC-1 only in that it has a different instruction set; otherwise it looks the same. DC-2 has the same "lift pen," "drop pen," "halt," and "go to x,y" instructions as DC-1. It has two additional instructions: one is the "add number e to location L" instruction, written "add e,L" and coded "4LLLL," followed on the next line by "eeeee"; the other instruction is "jump to location L" ("jump L"), which is coded "5LLLL." (See Figure 1-5.)

First let's consider the meaning of the "jump L" instruction. It is possible for player piano paper to be completely blank

DC-2

LP	10000
DP	20000
HLT	00000
GT x, y	3xxyy
JMP L	5LLLL
ADD E, L	4LLLL
	EEEEE

FIGURE 1-5. *The instruction set of DC-2 contains two instructions not found in the instruction set of DC-1: a "jump" instruction and an "add" instruction.*

paper on a roll. However, there may be advantages to supplying player piano paper with a grid printed on it. This grid would have numbered rows and columns; each square in the grid would have a unique location specified by two numbers, and we would easily be able to locate where to place holes when entering a tune into the player piano paper. The disadvantage of this scheme is that holes could not be placed just anywhere, as they can with a real player piano. Each instruction would consist of a row of holes, and each row would have a unique number, or *address*, by which that instruction could be located. Similarly, each instruction that you place in a computer memory is located by a specific address for that location.

When you place a list of instructions into a computer mem-

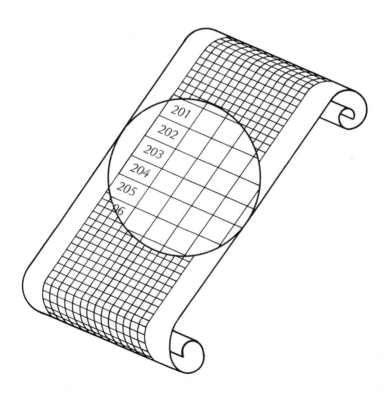

FIGURE 1-6. *We may artificially restrict the positions on player piano paper where holes may be punched.*

ory you have to decide where to put it, just as you have to decide where to start punching holes in a roll of player piano paper. In general, you can put it anywhere in the memory that you wish. Just as a roll of player piano paper might have 1,000 rows, and you could begin punching the holes for a tune at row 200, so a computer memory might have 1,000 locations for instructions, and you could begin putting instructions into a computer memory at location 200. The first instruction might go at location 200, the next instruction at location 201, and so on. Thus a program that is 10 instructions long (the last being a "halt") might begin at location 200 and end at location 209; or it could begin at location 500 and end at location 509. You can place it anywhere that you wish. The simple program that we wrote to draw a square would take up nine successive locations in the memory. It might begin at location 100 and end at location 108. To tell a computer where a program starts you would tell it the address of the first instruction in the list of instructions forming that program. This is in contrast to the way you would tell a player piano where to start taking instructions from a roll of paper: you would position the paper under the appropriate mechanism for reading the holes. The player piano has no mechanism for automatically locating paper at a particular numbered row.

In a player piano, if you know the number of the row that is being read by the player piano mechanism, you always know the number of the next row that is going to be read—it is simply the next one. A parallel situation generally exists in computers. Instructions are executed in order, the instruction in any one location being followed by the instruction in the next location. However, this is not always the case. The "jump" instruction in computers allows you to specify the address of the next instruction to be executed. For example, suppose a "jump" instruction is located at location 100 and it is an instruction that says to take the next instruction from location 1000; the instruction would be "jump 1000." First the instructions in location 90, 91, . . . , 98, 99, 100 would be executed. After that, the next instruction would be taken at location 1000, the next one at 1001, then 1002, and so on until another jump instruction was reached.

A program might start at location 100 and extend to location 109, where we would place a "jump 100" instruction. At this point the computer would go back to location 100 to take its next instruction. Thus the computer would be in a "loop," executing instructions 100 through 109 again and again, never stopping. This facility allows repetitive functions and can obviously be useful in a number of circumstances. If a player piano had this capability, it would be possible to use a "jump" instruction to repeat pieces of the composition without having to punch them many times into the paper.

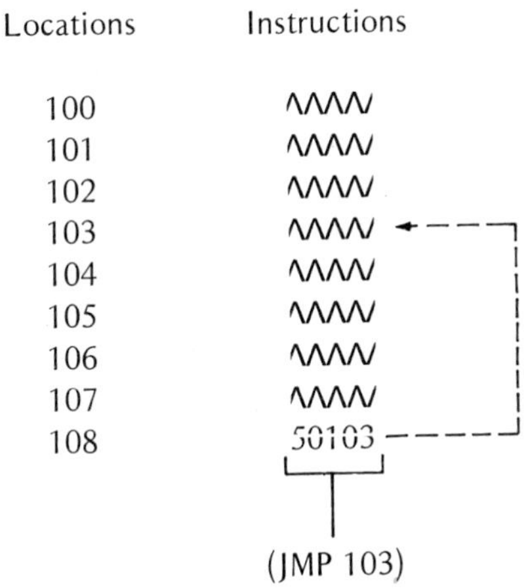

Locations	Instructions
100	∧∧∧
101	∧∧∧
102	∧∧∧
103	∧∧∧ ◄ - - - ┐
104	∧∧∧ ¦
105	∧∧∧ ¦
106	∧∧∧ ¦
107	∧∧∧ ¦
108	50103 - - - - ┘

(JMP 103)

FIGURE 1-7. *The "jump" instruction causes the central processing unit to "jump" to a place in the memory to get the next instruction.*

The "jump" instruction for DC-2 is coded "5LLLL." (In place of the four L's you would place a four-digit number specifying the address to which the program would jump.) Hence the instruction "50010" would jump to location 10, the instruction "50111" would jump to location 111 and so on. You can jump to any location between 0 and 9999.

Let us consider the "add" instruction. The "add" instruction in DC-2 allows you to add a number to the contents of a location and put the result back into that location. For example, if location 400 contained the number 30, and an instruction executed was "add 20,400," location 400 would contain 50 after instruction execution. The "add" instruction allows you to add to any location in the memory. That means that if your program is in the memory, the "add" instruction can modify your program.

The "add" instruction shows an important contrast between the memory and instructions of a computer and the memory and instructions of a player piano. The player piano has no capability for modifying the roll of paper containing its instructions. In contrast, instructions can and do modify the memory of a computer: the "add" instruction is just one example from this hypothetical machine, DC-2, but you can easily imagine kinds of instructions that would modify memory in other computers. (See Figure 1-8.)

Suppose that the memory of the computer contained two lists of numbers and a program for adding the corresponding elements in the two lists to form a third list with their sum. The program might be located beginning at location 100, the first list beginning at location 200, the second list beginning at location 300, and the third list beginning at location 400. (This list of sums would not exist until our program had been run. Until that time the locations beginning at location 400 would contain "random" numbers.) After we began our program it would modify the contents of locations following location 400, leaving the two original lists beginning at 200 and 300 unchanged. If we made a mistake in our program it might not create the third list of sums beginning at location 400 (as we wished), but at another location, say 1000. No great disaster would result, except that we might not be able to find our calculated results. However, what if the error were such as to create the list of sums starting at location 120—right in the middle of our program! The numbers that made up our program would be changed to others (the sums of the two lists) and these, being data rather than instructions, would not be properly interpreted by the central processing unit so as to complete the calculation of our list of sums.

Note that the "add" instruction requires two successive locations in the memory. When the central processor fetches the first words of the instruction ("4LLLL"), it will "know" that the 4 implies the "add" instruction, and that the "add" instruction is a two-word instruction. Before attempting to execute anything it will fetch the next word in the list of instructions, because without the next word it will not know what to add.

The decision of whether instructions will take up one or two words is based on the specific design of the instruction set and is determined by the computer manufacturer. The ability of the central processor to correctly fetch one or two words (sometimes more) is wired into the electronic design.

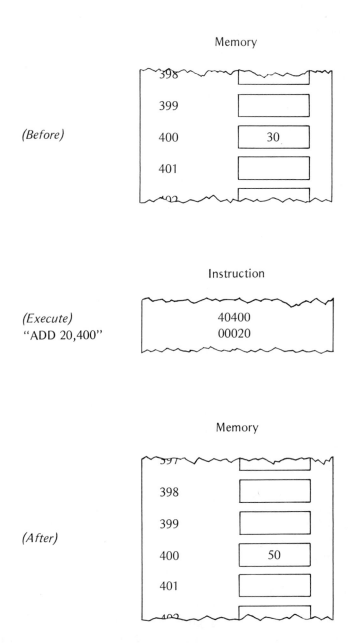

Memory

(Before)

398
399
400   30
401
402

Instruction

(Execute)
"ADD 20,400"

40400
00020

Memory

(After)

397
398
399
400   50
401
402

FIGURE 1-8. The "add" instruction allows you to modify the contents of any location in the memory.

15

There is an important lesson to be learned from the "add" instruction and its two-word length. The paper memory of a player piano has limited width, and so a limited amount of information can be punched into each row or into each instruction. Similarly, the locations in the computer memory, or, as they are sometimes called, "words," can contain a limited amount of information and are of limited length. For DC-1 and DC-2 I have arbitrarily set the length of the word at five digits. If I had wished to invent a more expensive computer, perhaps each individual word would be ten digits in length. If each word were ten digits in length, then the "add" instruction would require only one word. However, the ten-digit word would be more than enough for the other instructions in the instruction set, such as the "halt," "go to," and the like —each of which requires only five digits. What would be coded in the extra five digits of the ten-digit word? They would probably be wasted.

Now let's write a more interesting program using the powerful instruction set of DC-2. Let's begin this program at location 100 with a series of eight instructions that draw a square, just as before. Following this, let's have four instructions that add the number 101 to locations 101, 103, 104, 105, and 106. (It is simply coincidental that the number we are adding—101— is being added to locations with addresses approximately the same as its magnitude. We could have located the program to begin, for example, at location 2345 or any other arbitrary location.) You will note that by making the proposed modification we have changed the computer program. The last instruction will be a "jump" to location 100, the beginning of the program. Note that this program never halts because it never encounters a "halt" instruction. Every time you reach the end it will jump back to the beginning again. Since the program is being modified each time it goes through the loop, it does something slightly different each time.

The first time through the loop, in the first eight instructions, it draws a square. If we look at the activity of the "add" instructions that modify the program, we see that they change each of the "go to" instructions. For example, "go to 0,0" is modified to "go to 1,1"; "go to 50,0" is modified to "go to 51,1," and so on. Hence, we can see that the second time through the loop another square will be drawn that is one unit to the right and one unit above the first square. The third time through the program the "go to" instructions will have been modified again, and we'll get a third square that is two units to the right and two units above the first square, and so on. (See Figure 1-9.) This program will continue without stopping until the edge of the paper is reached, at which time manual intervention will be required to stop the process.

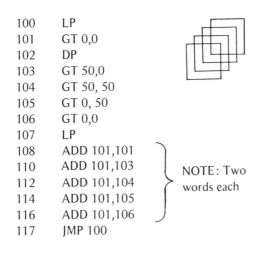

100	LP
101	GT 0,0
102	DP
103	GT 50,0
104	GT 50, 50
105	GT 0, 50
106	GT 0,0
107	LP
108	ADD 101,101
110	ADD 101,103
112	ADD 101,104
114	ADD 101,105
116	ADD 101,106
117	JMP 100

NOTE: Two words each

FIGURE 1-9. *This program would cause DC-2 to draw a series of squares, each displaced by one unit (inch, millimeter, or whatever) from the one drawn before. Because the "add" instructions are two words each, the numbers that would occupy locations 109, 110, 111, 113, and 115 would be the second half of the "add" instruction.*

Drawing Computer 2 is a useful computer. Who could have the patience and accuracy to draw squares just as it has done? Real computers frequently have instruction sets that are considerably more powerful than those of DC-1 and DC-2, and they can do more interesting and more complicated things.

This chapter has been concerned with an introduction to what computers do, or what they can do. Computers can solve any problems for which you can precisely state the solution. By "precisely state," I mean that you can define the solution exactly, and state it in the framework of the instruction set of the particular computer you are using. Different people may arrive at the same general solution for a problem, but the details of their solutions may differ. Therefore, the computer programs that they write may differ although the end results will be the same. You should not believe that there is a "correct" computer program to solve any particular problem, although computer programs do differ in speed of execution and general efficiency. Your job in using a computer is to specify the solution to your problem in the instruction set of the computer, write a program, translate the program into numbers, enter the numbers into the computer memory, and start the program at its starting location.

You have seen how one can translate a program written in the instruction set of a computer into numbers that the computer will understand. The rules are set up by the manufacturer. We have not yet discussed how to get numbers into the computer memory, how to position the computer to begin your program at the appropriate place, or how to start the computer. All computers have a variety of lights, switches, and buttons that control these operations, and the precise directions are supplied in a manual by the manufacturer.

2

HOW DO COMPUTERS
DIFFER FROM
OTHER MACHINES?

Computers differ from "ordinary machines" in that they have a memory, in which to store a set of instructions and data, and a central processing unit (CPU), to execute those instructions and to direct the operation of the machine. In addition, a computer contains *peripherals* such as typewriters, graphic displays, and the like, which interact with the users of the machine. The qualities of a computer may include ease of use and speed of operation. The characteristics of the memory and of the CPU, and the way in which the central processor, memory, and peripheral devices are connected are also factors that contribute to the qualities of a computer.

In describing the way a computer system is organized it is useful to think of the individual devices (CPU, memory, peripherals) as blocks, connected by paths for communication (Figure 2-1). The CPU must take information from the memory (instructions) and operate on it (execute the instructions). For the CPU to direct the operations of peripherals it is necessary to communicate with them. Since the CPU, memory, and pe-

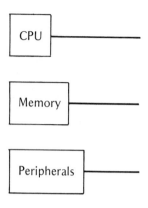

FIGURE 2-1. *The basic building blocks of a computer are the central processing unit, the memory, and the different kinds of peripherals.*

ripherals on all modern computers are electronic or electro-mechánical, the independent devices of a computer system are connected by wires. These wires do not differ in any significant way from those in other electronic machines, such as televisions or radios. Unfortunately, it usually takes many wires to connect two devices in a computer system, sometimes up to several hundred. These large collections of wires connecting devices are called *buses.* For our discussion of potential configurations of devices in a computer system it is acceptable to consider the individual pieces (the CPUs, memories, peripherals) as black boxes connected by wires. Each has a specific function: the CPUs fetch instructions and execute them; the memories contain numbers, which are sometimes used as instructions; and peripherals interact with the users of the computer system.

One simple configuration for a computer system is the *star configuration* (Figure 2-2), which enables computers to execute programs at high speed. Because buses can carry only a limited amount of information at any one time, the more buses there are in a system, the higher the potential rate of information transfer within that system. In the star configuration each device is connected to the CPU by a separate bus, so each device can be independently controlled, and many devices can be controlled simultaneously. Therefore, several peripherals can be doing useful tasks at the same time that the central pro-

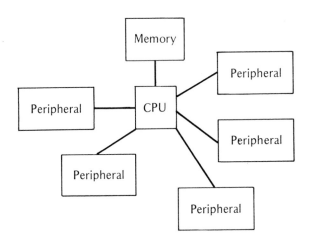

FIGURE 2-2. *In the* star configuration, *each peripheral and the memory are independently connected to the central processing unit.*

cessor is fetching and executing instructions from memory. The disadvantage of this configuration is that the central processor must be rather complicated in order to control a number of devices simultaneously, so it may be prone to breakage and will be quite expensive.

A second configuration as shown in Figure 2-3, does not require a complicated CPU because the central processor is

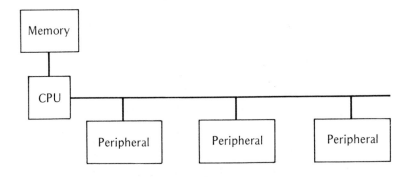

FIGURE 2-3. *With a single bus, only one peripheral can interact with the central processing unit at a time, and each can interact with memory only through the central processing unit.*

connected to only two buses—one goes to the memory and one goes to all the peripherals. The savings in initial cost of purchase of the central processor can be significant. However, this system has some obvious limitations. For one thing, the central processor can only communicate with a single device at a time. This does not mean that only one device can be working at any one time: if a peripheral does something that is very slow (such as a typewriter typing a character) then the computer can initiate the typing of the character and go on to deal with another peripheral while the typewriter is still doing the typing. As compared with the star configuration, this second configuration shows a decrease in speed when dealing with peripherals. In addition, there is no easy way for a peripheral to make a direct connection with the memory; if a peripheral gathers information for storage, all the information must flow through the central processor. Similarly, if you wish to move a large mass of information from the memory to a peripheral, it is necessary to go through the central processor. If the central processor is executing instructions and a need arises for a peripheral to communicate with the memory, the operation of the central processor must be interrupted. In an attempt to alleviate this last problem, a secondary path may be created from the memory to the peripherals (Figure 2-4). This allows considerably faster communication between the memory and the peripherals than previously possible. However, communication between the peripherals and the mem-

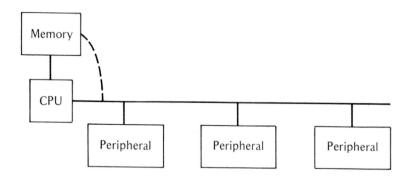

FIGURE 2-4. *An extra path may be provided between memory and peripherals, thus bypassing the central processing unit.*

ory may slow down the fetching of instructions by the central processor. The memory can deal with only one device at a time, and so it can either give instructions to the central processor or exchange information with one of the peripherals, but not both.

Although most memories cannot deal with more than one external device at a time, some, called *multiport memories*, are constructed to deal with two, three, or more devices at one time. That is, they can transfer numbers to or receive numbers from several devices simultaneously, and not limit the speed of any of them. The way this is accomplished, in most cases, is to divide the memory into small sections and to hope that no two devices will want to use the same section at one time. One approach would be to divide the list of locations into small parts, for example, "chunks" of 100 or 1,000 words. Hence, a memory might contain four 1,000-word pieces. As long as no two devices need to have access to the same 1,000-word piece, they can operate independently. For a computer with a multiport memory, therefore, it is important to write programs such that devices do not need access to the same piece of memory simultaneously. Sometimes, unfortunately, this is impossible, in which case the full power of a multiport memory cannot be realized.

The next configuration that we will consider is one in which there is a single bus to which all memory and peripherals are attached. Because all peripherals are attached to the same bus, their connections to the bus are similar, and there can be great savings in designing these interfaces (electronics connecting the peripherals to the bus). (See Figure 2-5.) Moreover, the

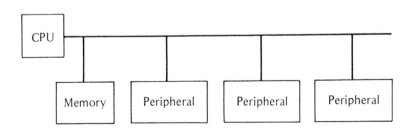

FIGURE 2-5. *When memory and peripherals are on the same bus, peripherals can obtain access to the memory at high speed.*

programs used to control the various peripherals are remarkably alike. There are serious disadvantages to this configuration: because all the devices are on one bus, the central processor can only deal with one of them at a time; furthermore, since the devices on the bus vary greatly in speed (one microsecond for memory to one-hundred-thousand microseconds for a typewriter) the bus cannot be optimized for any particular speed of device—it must accommodate the slowest and the fastest.

All buses to which two or more devices are attached have "traffic" problems. It is important that the devices do not try to use the bus at the same time and thereby confuse their messages. To this end, a *bus controller* is always attached to buses (Figure 2-6). Although the bus controller has not been

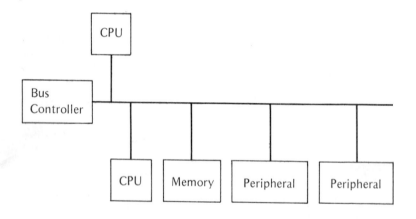

FIGURE 2-6. *With a sufficiently complex bus controller, two or more central processing units may coordinate their activities within a computer.*

shown in any of our configurations, we shall assume that it is present. The bus controller acts as a "traffic cop" to see that no two devices try to communicate on the bus at the same time. In the case of the single bus configuration, the bus controller is built into the central processor. Single bus configurations need not have the bus controller in the central processor.

Having the bus controller in the central processor may be a disadvantage if one wants to have two or more central processors in a system. For example, a configuration might consist of two central processors on the same bus, with memory and peripherals attached to this bus. In principle, this could give an increase of speed over the single bus–single central processor case because two central processors could be fetching and executing instructions from the memory. In order for the multiple CPU system to operate faster than its single CPU cousin, the limiting factor in the speed of the computer should be the execution of the instructions by the central processor. If, however, the limitation is getting information into and out of the memory, there will be no, or very little, increase in speed, because either or both CPUs will spend their time waiting for the memory to give them information.

As you can see, all the configurations we have discussed, with the exception of the star configuration, are potentially limited in their speed because of a lack of data paths. This can be overcome, to some extent, by combining two computers in a clever way. Consider a system that consists of two computers, each based on the single bus. The two buses are connected by way of a multiport memory (Figure 2-7). Each central processor executes programs contained in the memory on its own bus, but the data on which these programs operate may be contained in the multiport memory. One computer system can be gathering data and analyzing it while the other computer is doing serious calculations based on that data. In this configuration there is very little conflict between the two ma-

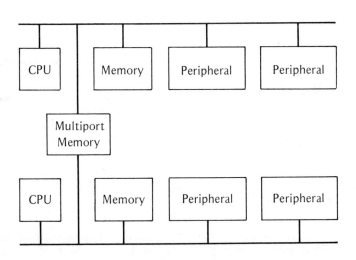

FIGURE 2-7. *With multiport memories, it is possible to connect two buses, and thus two computers, into one functional unit.*

chines, and the most serious question is one of coordination of their actions—a question that is certainly not trivial.

The specific configurations of computer systems to a large extent determine their "personalities." The configurations we have discussed by no means exhaust those that are possible or that are currently in existence. They are, however, examples of some of the most popular current configurations.

We have noted that many wires connect the pieces of a computer system, but we have not commented on how numbers can be transmitted along those wires. The only time numbers are transmitted along wires in our everyday experience is when we use the telephone. One possibility for computers would be that messages would be coded on wires the same way that the human voice codes them. Unfortunately, computers today cannot readily understand human speech, so this idea is not practical. Moreover, it takes about a half-second to transmit even the simplest number (one digit) by voice over a telephone wire: this rate of speed is much too slow to be useful in computer systems. Therefore we should consider another scheme.

One way we could transmit numbers would be to have a single wire connecting two devices. If one device wished to transmit a number to the other, it would put an appropriate voltage onto that wire. For example, if one device had to transfer the number 1,000, it could put 1,000 volts onto the wire (or 1,000 millivolts or 1,000 microvolts). If it wished to transfer the number 10 it could put 10 volts on the wire, and so forth. Whether the basic unit for transmission is volts, millivolts, or microvolts (or anything else), this system has some very real problems. For one thing, very small numbers will probably get lost in the noise on the wires. Because transmission on these wires meets interference, just as almost all electrical transmission on wires meets some interference, there will be a large error rate with small numbers. Similarly, in order to carry large numbers (millions or billions), it would be necessary to produce an electronic system capable of dealing with huge voltages, and the accuracy of this system would not be very great. All in all, the advantage of a single wire is unquestionably outweighed by the disadvantages.

Another possibility would be to connect devices by small numbers of wires—four, let us say, for an example. Each one of these wires would, at any time, carry 0 volts, 1 volt, 2 volts, ..., 8 volts, or 9 volts. With each of the four wires carrying an integral number of volts, the four wires together could code any number between 0000 and 9999. All that would be necessary would be to have electronic devices at the ends that could send and receive numerical information in this form. The noise problems would be eliminated because none of the voltages would be very small, there would be no problem of high voltages, and by adding more wires it would be possible to accommodate a number as large as we might like. The critical limitation with this scheme is the availability of fast, reliable, and inexpensive electronic devices to code and decode numbers in this form.

If the electronic decoding devices had fewer than ten possible choices they might be faster, cheaper, and more reliable. We may examine our motives and consider why we insist on connecting devices using multiple wires and a number transmission based on our base 10 arithmetic. (If you do not understand what base 10 arithmetic is, or binary and octal arithmetic, you should consult Appendix A at this time.) In fact, we could transmit numbers from one device to another on multiple wires using binary (base 2) arithmetic. In this case each wire would carry only two voltages, and electronics at either end would decode the two possibilities for each wire. Using a base 2 system rather than a base 10 system requires a larger number of wires, but wires are relatively inexpensive and easy to procure compared to high-speed, reliable electronic components for coding and decoding. The base 2 system is used for most computers.

With this introduction to computer system organization, it is worthwhile to consider the two devices in a computer system that are most alien to our prior experience—namely, the memory and the central processor.

The details of a central processor are too complicated for us to consider in this book. The central processor contains locations for saving instructions while they are being executed; it also contains *registers*, which are special storage locations that are capable of storing a single word. Many of the registers of the central processor cannot be modified by the user. One particular register in the central processor that is of great interest is called a *program counter* (PC). The program counter tells the central processor the location of the next instruction to be fetched from the memory and executed. That is, the program counter contains a number, an address; when the central processor has to fetch an instruction from the memory,

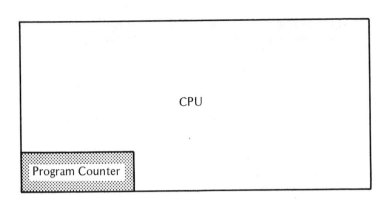

FIGURE 2-8. *The central processor contains a register—the program counter—which always contains the address of the next instruction to be executed.*

it fetches an instruction from the address that is contained in the program counter. Obviously, the program counter must be advanced from instruction to instruction, and so it must be incremented between instructions. This is the job of the central processing unit and need not concern the user. The central processing unit modifies the program counter so that it contains the address of the next instruction to be executed, regardless of whether or not the previous instruction was one or two words long. In fact, in some computers instructions are a variable number of words long, and yet the central processing unit properly addresses the program counter. The user of the computer must indicate where the program is located in the memory, that is, where it must start. This can be done by putting the address into the program counter and then starting the computer. The user of the computer can incorporate instructions into his program that modify the program counter: the "jump" instruction, for example, places a new number into the program counter.

Thus we see that there is a basic cycle to instruction execution (Figure 2-9). First, the central processor examines the program counter to learn the address of its next instruction. It then fetches that instruction. In some computers, the central processor increments the program counter to the address of the next instruction before it executes the instruction it has just fetched. It will then execute the instruction. The next step

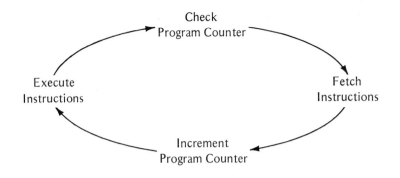

FIGURE 2-9. *Basic cycle for instruction execution.*

will be a return to the program counter for information about where the next instruction is located.

Let's work through two examples of actual programs for DC-2, showing how the instructions are executed and the program counter is modified. The first program draws a square and then halts. Let's assume that the instructions are placed in the memory beginning at location 100 and ending at location 108. (See Figure 2-10.) The steps to be followed are these:

    1. You load the number 100 into the program counter using switches, buttons, lights, etc., on the front of the ˙ computer.

    2. You start the computer by pressing a switch labeled "start," "begin," or the like.

100	LP
101	GT 0,0
102	DP
103	GT 50,0
104	GT 50,50
105	GT 0,50
106	GT 0,0
107	LP
108	HLT

FIGURE 2-10.

3. The central processor consults the program counter, sees that it contains the number 100, and takes from location 100 the instruction "lift pen," coded as number 10000.

4. The program counter is incremented so that it now contains 101.

5. The pen is lifted.

6. The central processor consults the program counter and sees that it contains 101; it goes to location 101 in the memory and gets the "go to 0,0" instruction.

7. The program counter is incremented to 102.

8. The pen moves to location 0,0.

9. The central processor consults the program counter, sees that it contains 102, and goes to the memory to fetch the "drop pen" instruction.

10. The program counter is incremented to 103.

11. The pen is dropped.

12. The central processor consults the program counter, sees 103, and fetches the "go to 50,0" instruction from location 103.

13. The program counter is incremented to 104.

14. The "go to 50,0" instruction is executed.

15. The central processor consults the program counter, sees 104, and gets the "go to 50,50" instruction from location 104.

16. The program counter is incremented to 105.

17. The "go to 50,50" instruction is executed.

18. The central processor consults the program counter, sees 105, and gets the "go to 0,50" instruction from location 105.

19. The program counter is incremented to 106.

20. The "go to 0,50" instruction is executed.

21. The central processor consults the program counter, sees 106, and gets the "go to 0,0" instruction from location 106.

22. The program counter is incremented to 107.

23. The "go to 0,0" statement is executed, thus completing the square.

24. The central processor sees 107 in the program counter, and fetches the "lift pen" instruction from location 107.

25. The program counter is incremented to 108.

26. The pen is lifted from the paper.

27. The central processor consults the program counter, sees 108, and takes the "halt" instruction from location 108.

28. The program counter is incremented to 109.

29. The "halt" instruction is executed.

For our second example, we will simply replace the "halt" instruction in location 108 with a "jump 100" instruction. At the end of the program we will have the following situation: the program counter will contain 108, and the central processor will execute the "jump location 100" instruction, which will place 100 into the program counter. The central processor will now consult the program counter to see where the next instruction is. Since the program counter contains the number 100, the next instruction will be taken from location 100 ("lift pen") and the program counter will automatically be incremented to 101. This cycle will continue indefinitely. In fact, the fetch-execute cycle continues until the "halt" instruction is reached, or until a natural catastrophe, such as an earthquake, strikes.

Now let us say a few words about the organization of a computer memory. It is functionally equivalent to a long roll of player piano paper—that is, it has two important dimensions: its width and its length. (See Figure 2-11.) The length is an expression of the number of words in the memory—that is, the number of numbers that can be stored in the memory. The smallest number of numbers that can be stored in the average computer memory is about one thousand, and the largest is about one million. The width of the memory reflects the maximum size of numbers that can be stored in any particular location. For a decimal computer, the width of the memory would indicate the number of digits that could be stored in an individual word. A comparable quality for binary

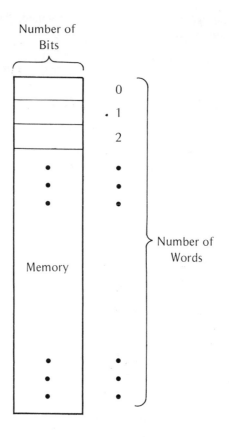

FIGURE 2-11. *Most memories are organized like a long strip of paper. Numbers can be written in a list anywhere on the paper, but each number can have only a limited width. If the numbers were decimal, they would be limited to a certain number of digits. Because they are binary, they are limited to a certain number of bits.*

computers is the number of bits that can be stored in a word —this is called the *word length*. Common word lengths include eight bits, twelve bits, sixteen bits, twenty-four bits, thirty-two bits, thirty-six bits, and sixty bits.

Generally, computer instructions manipulate whole words; they might, for example, move a word from one place to another. However, some computers also have instructions to modify parts of words or to deal with half-words.

Groups of eight adjacent bits within a word are occasionally referred to as *bytes*. Thus, a thirty-two-bit word may be said to contain four bytes. Some computers have instructions that enable them to manipulate individual bytes within a word.

The speed with which an individual word in the memory can be accessed differs according to the type of electrical components used. The smallest time commonly in use is about a tenth of a microsecond, and the largest time may be ten microseconds. This range of access time is accompanied by a wide range of costs. A small memory working at high speed might cost about the same as a large memory working at low speed. Large computer systems frequently have parts of their memories made of different components, and therefore they vary in speed. One can place parts of programs or data that require rapid access in a "fast" memory, and other parts of programs and data that do not require rapid access in a "slow" memory. With sufficient cleverness, such an arrangement can provide speeds of program execution comparable to a situation in which the entire memory is fast, with a considerable saving in cost over a memory that is entirely fast. One system of this sort is called the *cache system*. In computers with the cache system of memory, the central processing unit always communicates with a fast memory. When necessary, blocks of numbers from a slow memory are transferred to the small section of fast memory, known as the *cache*. Similarly, the numeric contents of the cache are transferred, when necessary, to locations in the larger slow memory. Despite the time necessary to make these block transfers of numeric information, some systems with a "cache" memory organization can operate at higher speeds than those without such an organization because the central processor does not have to wait as long for access to the memory with which it interacts.

The central processors and memories of computers are relatively simple devices. One fetches and executes instructions, and the other stores numbers, which may or may not be interpreted as instructions. The other parts of computer systems, namely peripherals of various sorts, are all common to our everyday experience. We may, therefore, inquire as to where the complexity and the mystery of computers come from; if all the devices are simple and if they are connected together in logical ways, why should the whole be a complex morass? As we shall see, the complexity shown by the behavior of any computer system is due almost entirely to the complexity of the programs that the computer system is executing. These, in turn, are products of the human mind, and reflect its complexity in posing and solving problems.

3

HOW DO PARTS OF COMPUTERS COMMUNICATE WITH EACH OTHER?

The unique features that set a computer system apart from most other machines are the central processing unit and the memory. However, a computer system that consists only of a central processing unit and a memory is not particularly interesting. It cannot interact with the outside world in any meaningful way. For instance, how useful would we find Drawing Computer 1 or Drawing Computer 2 if they did not have drawing arms? The peripherals, which do the useful tasks that we desire, are critical parts in a computer system.

This chapter collects some general observations about information transfer between devices in a computer system. We are particularly concerned with the ways that programs written by users of the computer system can control transfer of information, and thus can control the activity of peripheral devices. Chapter 4 consists of a collection of examples of peripheral devices that are commonly attached to computer systems.

It is useful to consider what exactly is transferred between devices in a computer system. At the level of physical description, an electron is transferred from one device to another. However, at the level of logical description, numbers are transferred. The wires connecting components of a computer system can carry binary-coded numbers from place to place. They can usually carry one word at a time. In a 16-bit computer, 16 bits of information comprising one word can be transferred from one device to another at one time. This is a *parallel transfer*. Other devices can transfer only one bit at a time along a bus, so it would take 16 times as long to transfer a word in a 16-bit machine using this "serial" method.

Just because only numbers can be transferred from one device to another does not mean that only numerical information can be transferred. We can make the numbers represent anything that we wish. One common choice is to have numbers represent letters.

To do this, we would decide on an acceptable character set and assign a number to each character. One character set might include the twenty-six letters of the alphabet, the ten digits 0 to 9, and several punctuation marks. Although in principle any numbers could be assigned to each of the characters in our character set, there are some established conventions. Generally, we use the lowest possible numbers in making assignments for each character. If our character set consisted of 26 possible characters, each one would be assigned a unique number between 0 and 25. Similarly, if our character set included 64 characters, each would be assigned a number between 0 and 63, and so on.

If there were only 2 characters in our character set, one bit would suffice to code these 2 characters. It might be "1" for the first character and "0" for the second character. If there were 3 characters in the character set, two bits would be necessary. In this case, there would be a waste because two bits can code 4 possibilities. If we use three bits we can code 8 possible characters, four bits can code 16 possible characters, five bits can code 32 possible characters, six bits can code 64 possible characters, seven bits can code 128 possible characters and eight bits can code 256 possible characters. A six-bit code is the smallest that is reasonable in order to accommodate letters, digits, and various punctuation marks. As more and more characters have been invented, a six-bit code has proved inadequate, so seven- and eight-bit codes are now commonly used.

The decision as to what number corresponds to what character is, to some extent, arbitrary. Individual users of a computer system do not have the option of choosing their own code—the various codes now in use have been chosen by international commissions. Since there have been several such commissions, contradictory codes are in existence and each computer system uses the one that the manufacturer has adopted.

If it takes, say, eight bits to code an individual character, it would be wasteful to code one character per computer word if the computer word were greater than eight bits. For example, if the computer word were sixteen bits long, two characters could be coded in each computer word, using an eight-bit code. The lower eight bits of the word could code one character, and the upper eight bits could code another character. When transferring information from place to place, it is useful to pack as many characters into a word as possible. This will mean that for a given list of characters fewer words will have to be transferred, and hence the transfer will take less time.

If the user of a computer wants a message to be typed on a Teletype, the characters comprising that message have to be moved to the Teletype. That is, instructions must be executed in a program to move each number representing the characters from the memory where they are stored to the Teletype. This, and similar data transfers, can be programmed in a number of ways. Each method of programming has its own advantages and disadvantages. Some methods are fast, some require few instructions, and others are simple to program. In all cases, the user must choose the appropriate instructions from the instruction set of the computer, arrange these instructions into a list that comprises his program, place the list, numerically represented, into the memory of the computer, and, finally, start it at the proper place.

One way that the user can program transfers of information from one device to another may be called the *word-by-word method*. In this case, specific instructions in your program initiate the transfer of each word from one device to another. Thus, if you want to transfer a thousand words you would need at least a thousand executed instructions. During transfer in a word-by-word mode, two processes are going on. One is that words are being transferred along the appropriate bus in the computer system. Another is that instructions are being fetched from the memory along a bus and executed by the central processor.

If one looks at a program to control the word-by-word transfer within a computer, it appears extraordinarily dull. The instructions are largely repetitive, and each one does just about the same as the last. Thus, it would appear possible to eliminate the fetching of instructions for such programs by building a piece of electronic equipment that could control the transfer.

We may inquire what information this piece of hardware would need in order to operate: it would need to know the number of words to be transferred, where the words are, and where they are going. Such devices do exist: they are special purpose interfaces built into some peripherals in a computer system. They contain registers, and it is the programmer's job to put into these registers the pieces of information the device needs to control the transfer. The interfaces can then control the transfer of a block of information from one device to another. While this special purpose interface is controlling the transfer, no instructions need be fetched from the memory and executed by the central processor to control or regulate the transfer. Thus, the central processor could wait for the job to be completed before continuing with the program, or it could go on and execute another section of the program that is unrelated to the transfer or that does not depend on its completion. In this case, we would again have two processes going on—a transfer of information and a fetching and execution of instructions. The program being executed by the computer would run at a lower speed than if no transfer were taking place because the memory can only deal with one process at a time: it must answer requests for information in the sequence in which they are received. Nevertheless, there is some saving in time, so the programmer of a computer system will frequently opt to run information transfer simultaneously with program execution.

Unfortunately, no two computers use the same methods to control the transfer of information from one device to another, so it is impossible to make generalizations about the instructions used for writing programs of this sort. We can, however, review the functions of programs that control the transfer of information. Such programs must select the devices involved in the transfer and they must be able to control the transfer by starting it, stopping it, and the like. Programs that control information transfer must also be able to determine, at any time, the status of the devices involved in transfer. For example, the program must be able to determine whether a typewriter is ready to receive a new character to print, or whether it is busy printing the previous character; or it may be necessary to determine whether or not a magnetic tape drive is moving. This status information must be supplied by the individual devices, and instructions must be available in the instruction set of the computer to determine such information. It is also necessary for the program to transfer information to the devices. In the word-by-word transfer mode, the actual data is transmitted. In the case of devices that can control block transfers, the program must transfer into registers in the devices information as to where the numbers are, where they are going, and how many numbers are involved. These registers are similar to the registers in the central processing unit, and while the transfer is in progress they hold information that is used by the electronic logic of the individual devices to determine what actions should be taken.

When dealing with a device that can control block transfers, the programmer has two options: he can have his program wait until the transfer is complete, or he can go on and execute a part of his program that does not depend on the completion of the transfer. In either case it may be necessary for the programmer to know when the transfer is finished. The device must gain the attention of the central processing unit to indicate that it has completed its job. Upon completion of the transfer, the programmer may wish that some action, in the form of a list of instructions, be executed. This would call for the device that controls the transfers, on completion of its job, to start a small program that has been assigned to "handling" the event of the job's completion. In fact, there is a more general problem hidden here: devices may need to gain the attention of the central processor for a number of reasons, thus requiring the central processor to execute short programs designed for treating individual devices. We would not want the central processor to spend most or all of its time waiting for requests for attention from devices—we would prefer that it execute a program while it is waiting.

When individual devices request the attention of the central processor, they must not only cause initiation of a program to handle their request, but they must also store information about what the processor had been doing so that the processor can resume operation after attending to the requesting device. Devices that are capable of gaining the central processor's attention when it is executing a program are said to "interrupt" the central processor.

The interrupt capabilities of devices are determined by the

design and construction of the computer. When a device wishes to interrupt the central processor, it sends an electric pulse on special wires, which triggers the following series of events:

1. The program being executed by the central processor is halted.

2. The address of the next instruction to be executed by the central processor is saved—where it is saved depends on the individual computer.

3. A new program is begun. This program is written by the user specifically to handle the case of an interrupt for a particular device.

When the interrupt program is completed and we want to restart the program that was interrupted, we return to the program counter the address that was previously saved. To take a specific example, suppose there are two programs in the memory, a main program and a program to handle the interrupt of a particular device. Both programs have been written by the user and placed into memory. The main program starts at location "s," and the program to handle the interrupt starts at "b." The main program runs until it is interrupted. Assume that it is interrupted just before it was to execute an instruction at location "a." The number "a" is then saved, and the number "b" is automatically placed in the program counter. Therefore, the CPU will execute instructions beginning at location "b." When the end of the interrupt-handling program is reached, instructions placed in this program by the user cause the number "a" to be returned to the program counter, so that execution of the main program is resumed at "a" as if the main program had never been interrupted.

Various types of events could have caused the interrupt. For example, some time between "s" and "a" the main program may have initiated a block transfer, and the interrupt just before "a" could indicate the end of that transfer.

This description of interrupt capability of the computer leaves a number of questions unanswered. What happens if the processor is in the middle of executing an instruction when the interrupt occurs? In that case, the processor is allowed to finish the instruction it is executing before the interrupt takes

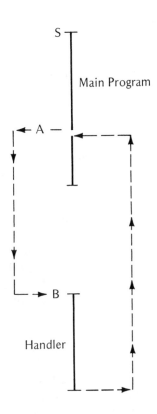

FIGURE 3-1. *The main program may be interrupted by a device when it is executing an instruction located at address "A." A second program to "handle" the interrupt may be located beginning at address "B."*

place. Where is the address stored to which the central processor will later return? This differs from machine to machine. In some computers, it is saved in location 0 of the memory; in others, it is saved in a special register that is in the central processor. There are a number of additional schemes. In all cases, the instruction set of the computer must provide for returning the address from where it was saved to the program counter at the end of an interrupt-handling program.

What happens if two or more devices try to interrupt the central processor at the same time? Again, this depends on the particular computer. In some cases, the device closest to the central processor along a bus is given priority; the farther device is temporarily ignored. In other systems, each device in the system is given a numerical priority, perhaps somewhere between 0 and 7, and in the case of conflict, the device with the highest priority will take precedence. These priorities may be set by the user of the computer if they have not been set by the manufacturer of the particular device.

If several devices can interrupt the central processor, and if each requires a unique handling program to be written and placed in the memory by the user, how will the central processor know which of the handling programs to start and where it is located in the memory? No simple answer can be given at this time, for the schemes used in the various computers differ greatly and are frequently rather complicated. Nevertheless, it is possible for the user to have handler routines for several interrupts arbitrarily placed in the memory. If everything has been set up correctly by the user, the proper choice of handling routine will be made.

What happens if an interrupt occurs while the central processor is running a program that handles a prior interrupt? Well, an interrupt-handler routine can be interrupted just as the main program can be interrupted. As before, the address of the next instruction to be executed will be saved and the new handling routine will be started. When the handling routine for the second interrupt is completed, the central processor will return to the first handling routine where it had been interrupted. This, in turn, will run to completion, and then the central processor will return to the main program at the proper location.

Let us consider a computer in which the return address is saved in location 0. If an interrupt occurs while another interrupt is being handled, the new return address will also be saved in 0, thus destroying the old return address and making it impossible to return to the proper place in the main program. There are a number of ways to solve this problem, but they are too complicated to discuss here.

Interrupts make it possible for the central processor to execute useful parts of a program while external devices are active. When the external devices require the attention of the central processor, they can interrupt it. However, an interrupt structure of a computer could easily turn into a nightmare if there were not some way for a programmer to control it through his program. For example, who would want a running program to be interrupted, and potentially destroyed, by someone tripping and falling against the Teletype, hitting a key and causing an inadvertent interrupt? Because of dangers of this sort, there are various controls on the interrupt capabilities of the computer that the programmer can incorporate into his program. Some computers have instructions that enable and disable all possible interrupts from any device. If the instruction to disable the interrupt is fetched from a program and executed by the central processor, no device can interrupt the execution of programs. By executing the appropriate instruction, however, a previously disabled interrupt can be enabled to interrupt the central processor.

Such instructions are obviously useful, but they are not very specific because they disable interrupting capabilities of all devices. Some computers have the capability of disabling the interrupts of certain devices while leaving others enabled. They have instructions capable of enabling or disabling the interrupt of specific devices in the computer system.

We can find a third control for the interrupt of a computer system by expanding our ideas with regard to device priority. Each device in a computer system may have a priority assigned by the manufacturer and built into the electronics. In some computers it is possible for the central processor to have a priority. If any device with a priority lower than or equal to that of the central processor attempts to interrupt it, the interrupt will be ignored. Devices with higher priority, however, can interrupt the central processor. Computers with this facility have the ability, through special instructions, to change the priority of the central processor. Hence, the program can protect itself from interruptions by certain devices, and leave itself open to interruption from certain other devices. You could write instructions in a program that would turn on or off all interrupts, enable or disable interrupts of specific devices, or assign a specific priority to the running program.

We've learned three things about the devices in a computer system:

1. Although all devices in a computer system deal exclusively with numbers, the numbers can represent anything we wish.

2. Some devices interact with others in the computer system by way of individual numbers or blocks of numbers, and the transfer of each number must be controlled

by the program that is executed by the central processor. However, more complicated and intelligent devices can control the transfer of blocks of numbers without the need of instruction execution by the central processor.

3. Many devices in a computer system have the ability to interrupt the central processor when they demand attention. Under such circumstances, it is the job of the central processor to execute a program to handle the request of the device. This program must be supplied by the user of the computer system, although it is always possible to borrow one from another programmer.

4

HOW DO COMPUTERS COMMUNICATE WITH PEOPLE?

Computers without peripherals are like brains without bodies —interesting curiosities. In contrast to our bodies, we have complete control over the characteristics of the peripherals attached to computer systems. A number of useful types have been developed.

It would be delightful if we could communicate with computers via the spoken word. If we could talk to computers and computers could talk to us, an efficient interactive exchange could be set up. Unfortunately, computers currently in use do not understand or produce very much human speech. The next best thing is to communicate via alphabetic or numeric characters. Peripherals have been produced that can receive a succession of characters from humans (by hitting the keys on a keyboard), and deliver those characters to a computer. On the other side of the coin, the central processor of a computer, by executing a program written by a user, can deliver a sequence of characters to devices that can then transform them to a typewritten message.

The first peripheral we will consider, one of the simplest and most common, is the typewriter. Common typewriters cannot easily be interfaced to computers, because they are not based on a numerical representation—they use a mechanical representation for each letter. There are many typewriters available that can interface with computers, the most common of which is the Teletype, so frequently seen in newsrooms around the world (Figure 4-1).

The critical difference between an everyday typewriter and the Teletype is that a Teletype uses a numerical representation for each character. When you hit a key on the keyboard of the

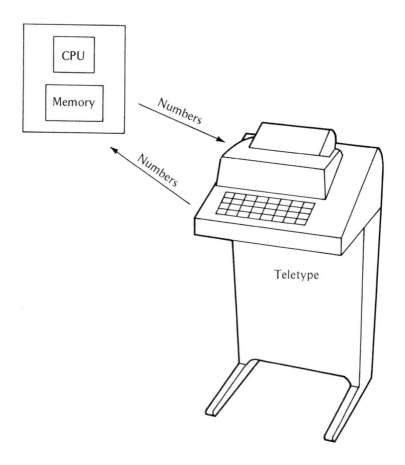

FIGURE 4-1. *Computers interact with peripheral devices, such as Teletypes, by transferring numbers to and from the devices.*

Teletype, a binary number is produced, electrically represented on wires, and this number can be read by the central processor of a computer. Similarly, the central processor of a computer can send, along wires, a number to the Teletype, which in turn will print the appropriate character. The Teletype cannot distinguish words and numbers that are meaningful from the gibberish that might be produced by the proverbial "monkey at the typewriter": analysis of the character input on a Teletype is left to a program in the computer that must be written by the user. A typical program might, for example, take in from the Teletype a string of characters that form the basis for a command. It might check the string of characters to make sure there were no syntactic errors in describing the command and then carry out whatever was desired. A Teletype will not type anything unless told to do so on a character-by-character basis by the central processor. Despite these limitations, Teletypes are extremely useful if controlled by a well-written program. They translate the input and output of material into intelligible form. Their main limitation is one of speed—they can type only ten to fifteen characters per second, although computers can produce results at a much higher rate.

A higher rate of output can be achieved by attaching a printer to a computer as a peripheral. A printer prints an entire line of text at one time, rather than a single character at a time as a Teletype does. This means that a program has to direct the central processor to move characters to the printer before the printer actually does anything. Where do these characters go? Most printers contain a small memory that can hold several characters. This memory will be successively filled by the central processor until an entire line of text has been assembled. At this time, the central processor will direct the printer to print what is held in its small memory, which is called a *buffer*. Printers range in speed from about 100 lines per minute to about 6,000 lines per minute. At the high end of the scale, they probably produce more information than we could ever hope to read.

Although a printer does a lot to get information out of a computer at a high rate of speed, it does nothing to improve the speed of getting information into the computer; this is the function of the so-called IBM card. This card contains information in the form of perforations that are similar to the holes punched in player piano paper. The holes are punched by people on card punches, and they represent a numerical code that can be read by a device known as a *card reader*. Card readers read a stack of punched cards, translate the holes into corresponding numbers, and the numbers can then be read by the central processor under the control of the program. Card readers can operate at speeds up to 1,000 or more cards per minute.

Intermediate in speed between Teletypes and printers/card readers are a group of devices for punching holes in paper tape, and for reading paper tape with holes punched in it. Binary numbers can be coded by the proper placement of holes in the paper tape. For example, holes may be placed in a row across the paper tape corresponding to the individual bits of a word, or a part of a word. Unless we are very well trained, we cannot read paper tape directly and make any sense of the characters that it represents. Hence, we should not expect punched paper tape to be an efficient high speed output mechanism for human consumption. On the other hand, punched paper tape is a useful intermediate storage medium. Since memories of all computers are limited, there may be occasions when we have too many numbers to store in the memory. In such cases, we can punch those numbers we don't need into paper tape. At a later time, a program can read the paper tape and reinstate the numbers in the memory. Paper tape is one of several media used for storing numbers when they are not needed in the memory of a computer. One advantage of paper tape is that the devices for punching it and reading it are extremely inexpensive. Unfortunately, paper tape readers and punches are not the most highly reliable storage media.

Magnetic tape is a faster and more reliable, although somewhat more expensive, storage medium. Magnetic tape and magnetic tape recorders used with computers as peripherals are similar to those used for some home high-fidelity systems. The tape is a little wider, the tape drive is of considerably higher quality, and the electronics are set up to store numbers rather than sounds. As with all peripherals, operation of the device is totally or largely under control of the program written by the user of the system. When magnetic tape is used, the program has to move words to the magnetic tape drive to store them or from the magnetic tape drive to read them. If the magnetic tape system has a capability for block transfer of words, the program must set up this transfer by indicating the number of words to be transferred and the location of the list of numbers, and it must initiate the transfer.

Although magnetic tape is very useful, it does have one serious disadvantage: the tape itself is long and narrow. Because of this, only a small amount of information can be stored in an individual row, and there are many rows along the length of the tape. Hence, if one is reading or writing numbers at one end of the tape, it takes a long time to get to the other end—the whole roll of tape must be wound or rewound. One way this problem could be reduced would be to have a continuous long loop of tape. In that case, the two ends would be adjacent. This scheme, however, is infrequently used.

Discs are peripherals that are used for storage of numbers and they do not have the access problems of magnetic tape. They are usually made of metal, shaped like frisbees, although a bit larger, and are covered on one or both sides with a metal oxide coating, similar to the metal oxide coating on magnetic tape. Numbers are coded along circular tracks, and a given disc may have 100 or 200 or more such tracks. (See Figure 4-2.) Because it is continuously rotating, the longest time necessary to read or write any number is the time for one full revolution of the disc—a few milliseconds in most systems. Such discs are called *fixed head discs*. Each track on the disc is assigned its own individual *head*, which is a device for magnetizing and

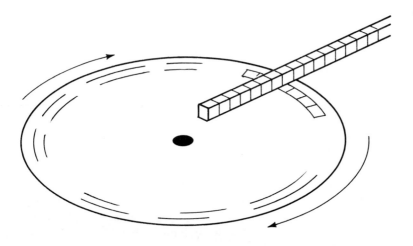

FIGURE 4-2. *A disc spins beneath a fixed row of magnetic reading and writing heads. Specific points on the disc are magnetized; the heads can magnetize points or read which points are magnetized.*

demagnetizing points on the track or for measuring those points on the track that are magnetized.

So far we have considered two classes of devices in the computer system: one is for communication between the user and the system—Teletypes, printers, card readers, and the like; the other is for temporary storage of numbers that are not needed in the memory of the computer—paper tape readers and punches, magnetic tape drives, and discs. With the capabilities these devices provide, computers can excel at problem solving.

We should also remember that computers are extraordinarily persevering. Once a program is started, it will run indefinitely unless stopped in one of several ways. It would be possible to program a computer in order to control some running process—a manufacturing plant, for example. To this end, it is desirable for computers to be able to turn things on and off. It would be possible to control a manufacturing plant by having the computer print, on a Teletype, instructions to a human operator, who would then follow those instructions. The concept of direct computer control has a number of advantages in that computers never go to sleep, make mistakes, take coffee breaks, or demand higher wages. Occasionally, they do break down, but so do human workers.

The binary representation of information in a computer system is admirably suited for on-off control of things. Since each bit of a word in the memory is either on or off (1 or 0) at any time, it would appear possible to connect each bit of a particular word, or several words, to machines. When those bits were on (1), the machines would be turned on; when those bits were off (0), the machines would be turned off. Thus, in a sixteen-bit computer, sixteen independent on-off decisions could be controlled by a single word. For technical reasons, it is difficult or impossible to connect wires directly to the individual bits of words in the memory. It is possible, however, to add to the computer system a peripheral that essentially consists of a single register to store a binary number with wires coming out of each bit. The central processor, under program control, can move numbers into the register, and each number will have particular bits on and particular bits off; that is, the wires connected to that register will either have 0 volts or some other voltage, say $+5$ volts, depending on the number in the register. These wires with their unique voltages can be connected to relays, switches, and the like, so machines can be directly controlled. (See Figure 4-3.)

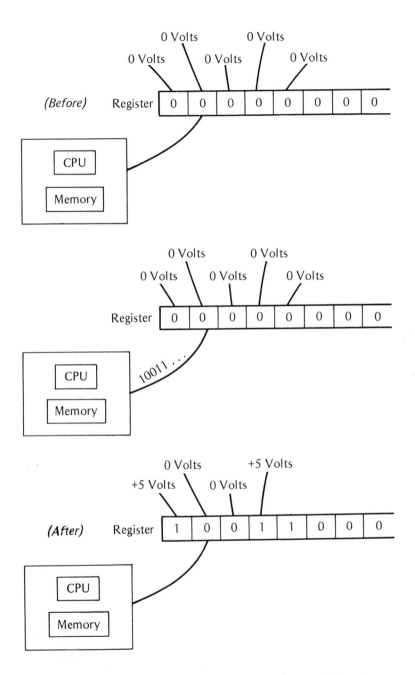

FIGURE 4-3. Wires can be connected to the individual bits of a register. When we move a number into the register, each bit will be 0 or 1. Corresponding to this, each wire will have one of two possible voltages—say, 0 volts or +5 volts. These voltages can be used to turn on or turn off devices.

The control of some devices requires more than a simple on-off decision. For example, in a chemical plant, it is not sufficient to open or close a valve; one must be able to control how "open" the valve is. In order to deal with these situations, peripherals have been developed that can produce a range of voltages. Such devices involve a lot of electronics, and include a register. The central processor moves numbers into the register, and the device produces voltages that are proportional to the number in the register. For example, if one moved the number 0 into such a register, 0 volts would be produced by the device and would be available on a wire extending from the device. Alternatively, if one put the number 1,000 into the device, it is possible that 10 volts would be produced on the wire: with the number −1,000, −10 volts would be produced. Any number between +1,000 and −1,000 would produce voltages between +10 volts and −10 volts. Such devices are called *digital-to-analog converters*, or D-to-A converters (Figure 4-4). Obviously, D-to-A converters cannot really produce a continuous range of voltages because discrete numbers must be placed in the register. In the example given, there are approximately 2,000 possible numbers that can be placed in the registers. Similarly, there are only 2,000 possible voltages that can be produced between −10 volts and +10 volts. Any voltage we want can be produced by such a D-to-A converter, but with an accuracy of only .01 volts (20 volts divided by 2,000 steps).

Although D-to-A converters provide the ability for a com-

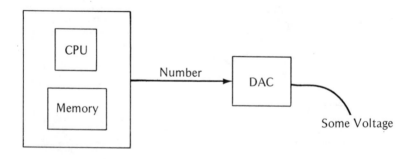

FIGURE 4-4. *A digital-to-analog converter (DAC) receives numbers from the computer and translates these into a voltage produced on a wire.*

puter, under program control, to control complex activities, we still have no efficient way of getting information into the computer, except in the form of numbers. In fact, we never will have a more efficient way, because a digital computer can operate only with numbers. It would be most useful, however, if we could convert certain things into numbers without human intervention, such as the intensity of light, temperature, amount of rotation, for example. Without converters for such things, computers must rely on human beings. The computer operator must measure a quantity and then enter the numerical representation into the computer by using a Teletype or card reader.

To avoid this, we might build a light-to-number converter. Whenever a light shines on this converter, the converter would produce a number that could be read by the central processor of the computer. The number would be proportional to the intensity of the light. Such a device, placed on the stage of a modern theater, would measure the amount of light on the stage and give this information to a computer, which could, by using D-to-A converters, control the light shining on that part of the stage.

If we think of the many things we wish to convert to numbers, the problem of designing individual devices for each one appears to be overwhelming. Fortunately, our technology has already approached this problem, but in a slightly different way. Converters or transducers that convert a number of things, such as light intensity, into electrical signals are presently available. For light, the electrical signal produced is a voltage proportional to the intensity of the light. Similar transducers are available for sound intensity, temperature, and many other things. The job is simplified by a device called an *analog-to-digital (A-to-D) converter*, which converts electrical voltages into numbers (Figure 4-5). This device is, in many ways, the opposite of the D-to-A converter. Into it goes a wire on which we may put any voltage we want to have measured. Out of it go several wires containing the binary representation of a number proportional to the voltage on the input wire. For example, a voltage of 0 on the input wire might produce the number "0." A voltage of 10 volts on the input wire might produce the number "+1,000." A voltage of 5 volts on the input wire might produce the number "500." As with the D-to-A converter, a limited range of voltages can be accommodated with limited accuracy.

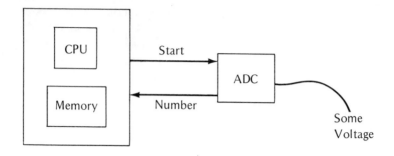

FIGURE 4-5. *An analog-to-digital converter (ADC) converts a voltage on a wire to a number, which is then delivered to the computer. This process takes place when the computer starts the conversion by the ADC.*

Analog-to-digital converters are completely under the control of the central processor, which in turn does nothing more than execute a user's program. A program to use an A-to-D converter would entail: (1) starting the A-to-D converter so that a conversion could be made, and (2) reading the results produced by the A-to-D converter, perhaps moving the number into the memory. A computer system might contain several A-to-D converters, so that voltages on many lines could be measured simultaneously. Because measurement of a voltage takes some time—several microseconds in most systems—it may not be possible to accurately measure a rapidly changing electrical signal. For example, when a sound enters a microphone it produces a rapidly changing electrical signal. It might be necessary, for a high-pitched sound, to measure the voltage produced 20,000 to 30,000 times per second in order to get an accurate representation. If such measurements were continued for any period of time, many numbers would be produced and these probably could not be stored in the memory of the computer. However, they could be stored on a disc or magnetic tape if the particular computer system in use had them.

Plotters are peripherals that produce straight lines on paper. A plotter consists of an arm and a pen; the arm can be moved in arbitrary straight lines. Just as DC-1 and DC-2 (chapter 1) made it possible for the programmer to control the drawing of any picture, so can a plotter draw any picture that can be programmed. The only real limitation on its performance is speed—the arm cannot move very fast. Other methods have been developed to increase the speed of picture drawing by computers.

All of the "graphic displays" that we will discuss in this chapter make use of a *cathode-ray tube* (CRT) of which the most common example is the television picture tube. The cathode ray tube is a glass vacuum tube. (See Figure 4-6.) At one

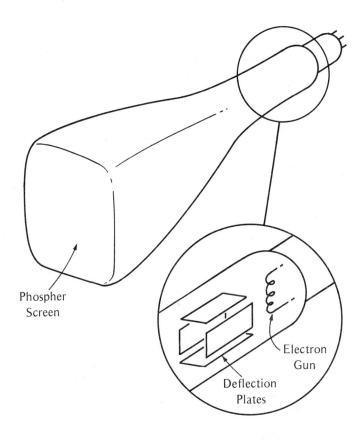

Phospher
Screen

Electron
Gun

Deflection
Plates

FIGURE 4-6. *A cathode ray tube (CRT) is similar to a television tube. Pictures are drawn on its face under computer control.*

end of the tube is an electron gun, which consists of a piece of wire that is heated by passing an electric current through it. When the gun is heated, electrons shoot out in all directions.

The electron gun is surrounded by a gadget that concentrates moving electrons into a narrow beam; this narrow beam shoots across the cathode ray tube and strikes the opposite side, which is coated with a phosphorescent chemical. The chemical glows wherever and whenever the electron beam strikes it. The glowing stops when the electron beam is turned off.

By turning on the electron beam (heating up the wire) we can produce a spot of light on the screen of the tube. By turning off the beam, we are able to turn off this spot of light.

We can make the cathode ray tube useful by adding two pairs of metal plates: one pair to surround the beam in the vertical direction, and the other pair to surround the beam in the horizontal direction. By putting electrical charges on these plates (connecting a voltage between the plates, similar to a battery), it is possible to divert the beam from its straight and narrow course. We can control the direction of the beam by putting the proper voltages on the vertical and horizontal plates, thus producing a spot of light wherever we wish for as long as we wish. If a computer has two D-to-A converters, one can be attached to the vertical plates and one can be attached to the horizontal plates, and by moving the proper numbers into the two D-to-A converters, voltages can be produced that will control the beam for us (Figure 4-7). For example, a short program could move numbers into D-to-A converters that would cause the beam to be deflected to the upper right-

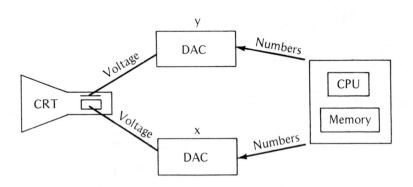

FIGURE 4-7. *A computer can produce two independent voltages by means of two digital-to-analog converters. Each can be connected to the horizontal or vertical deflection plates of a cathode ray tube and can move the electron beam to any point on the face of the CRT.*

hand corner of the tube, so we would see a spot of light in the upper right-hand corner. Another program might move the beam to the lower left-hand corner. By combining these two programs, we could alternately move the beam to the upper right-hand corner and then to the lower left-hand corner, and back again. The high speed of the computer and the D-to-A converters would make it appear as if there were two points—one in each corner, rather than a single point of light moving between the two corners. We can use this procedure to produce three, four, or more points on the screen at one time. Most computers can move the beam sufficiently rapidly that there appear to be thousands of points on the screen at any one time. With several thousand points, it is possible to draw a rather complicated picture.

A comparison between a plotter and a CRT display is useful. The plotter can produce a picture of any complexity we desire, because there is no serious speed limitation, but the CRT display does have an upper limit to the complexity of picture it can produce before the picture begins to flicker. On the other hand, the time it takes to produce a moderately complex picture on a CRT is much lower than the time it takes to plot a moderately complex picture on paper.

In an effort to speed up the production of points in a CRT display, and thus increase the complexity of picture that can be produced without a flicker, special devices have been constructed. One of the most interesting is a *vector generator* (Figure 4-8). The vector generator is a device that draws

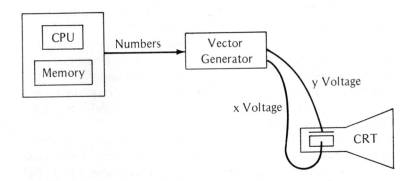

FIGURE 4-8. *A vector generator accepts numbers from the computer and produces two variable voltages that move the electron beam of the CRT in such a way as to draw a straight line. A tablet converts the position of a pen on a surface to two numbers that are transmitted to the computer.*

straight lines on the face of the CRT. It interfaces with the computer and receives instructions from the CPU to the computer. These instructions tell the vector generator where to start drawing a line and where to end it. Such information requires at least four numbers—two coordinates for the beginning and two coordinates for the end of the line. When the computer makes this information available to the vector generator, the vector generator will draw the line without further control from the computer. A vector generator can draw about 100 times faster than a computer that uses D-to-A converters. A computer that controls a D-to-A converter can directly produce a picture that contains several thousand points, and if the points are close together, it can look as if a line has been drawn. The total length of line that can be kept on a screen by the computer without noticeable flicker is only a few inches (10 or 20). However, a vector generator under computer control can produce a picture containing 1,000 or 2,000 inches of line.

Special devices have also been built to draw circles and produce characters on a CRT screen at considerably higher speeds than possible if the computer directly controls D-to-A converters.

A picture will flicker when the computer cannot repetitively produce the points making up the display at a sufficiently high rate. The phosphor of a CRT screen only glows when actually being hit by electrons; it does not continue to give off light after the beam has moved to another position, so in order to keep a point on the screen it is necessary to repeatedly move the electron beam to that position. This problem has been solved, in part, by the development of a phosphor that continues to glow after the electron beam has moved to another position. Cathode ray tubes that have such phosphors are called *storage tubes*. If a computer uses a storage tube, it does not need a vector generator, character generator, or circle generator because the picture will remain almost indefinitely after having been drawn only once.

We may inquire as to the cost of storage tubes, for it may appear that they can be used to draw one picture but then can never be used again, just like paper. Actually, this is not true: It is possible to "erase" a storage tube, electrically, so that old information in the phosphor is lost and a new picture can be drawn.

Storage tubes do not provide an answer to all of our graphic problems. If a picture is drawn on a storage tube and a small part has to be changed, the entire picture must be erased and a new picture must be drawn. In contrast, a non-storage tube makes it possible to change only part of a picture, or to change it slightly without massive overhaul.

The ability to make small changes in displays makes possible "dynamic" displays—in which objects produced by the computer on the CRT screen appear to move. The principle behind this is exactly the same as with movies. A picture is drawn again and again, and each version is slightly different from the last. Thus, we can get apparent movement on a CRT screen, but we cannot get apparent movement on a storage tube screen.

Each system has its advantages. With a storage tube, it is not necessary to use an expensive vector generator, character generator, or circle generator. We can produce a picture as complex as we like at high speed. With a non-storage tube, it is possible to produce moving images, and, for some applications, this is critical.

The output of a plotter is a picture on paper, and we can store this picture for as long as we like. In contrast, the output of a CRT display is rather ephemeral; it disappears as soon as the computer is turned off or the program ends. A number of approaches have been tried in order to get "hard copy" from a CRT display—that is, to get a copy of the picture on paper. Unfortunately, essentially all methods currently in use are either very expensive or produce low-quality output. At the present time, the best solution appears to be to take a photograph of whatever is on the screen.

The graphic displays described allow the user of a computer to write programs that will cause the central processor to draw a variety of complex pictures. We might also inquire whether it is possible to get picture information into a computer. In fact, a number of devices for doing this exist, and we will consider one of them—a peripheral known as a *tablet* (Figure 4-9). A tablet is flat and its area may measure approximately one square foot. A special pen is attached to it, and both the pen and the tablet are attached via an electronic interface to the computer. The important part of the interface consists of two registers—an x register and a y register, which contain numbers that represent the x coordinate and the y coordinate of the pen if it is placed on the tablet. The user can lift the pen and point to any place on the tablet; by reading numbers

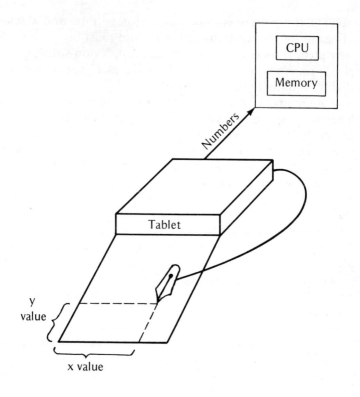

FIGURE 4-9. *A tablet enables the user to measure x and y coordinates.*

from the two registers, a program can know where the user is pointing. (Note that this device in no way acts as a graphic display.) The x and y coordinates so measured could be disposed of by the program, transformed in a variety of ways, or, if you wished, moved to the two D-to-A converters that control the graphic display. By measuring the coordinates of the pen and storing a list of these coordinates, it is possible for the computer to measure curves drawn by a user, store these curves for later use, and retrieve them for display whenever necessary.

5

WHAT INSTRUCTIONS
DO COMPUTERS
FOLLOW?

INSTRUCTION SETS

We have studied the organization of devices within a computer system (memory, CPU, and peripherals) and the types of peripherals that can be attached to a general computer. Both the organization and the choice of peripherals determine the "personality" of the computer. Two additional important characteristics are the type of instruction set the computer has and the way this instruction set can be used in order to write organized programs. In this chapter we will consider samples of different kinds of instruction sets and the way individual instructions are organized to give the central processor sufficient information so that it knows what to do. We will also consider ways in which the user of a computer might organize the instructions in his program so as to gain flexibility, avoid obsolescence, and allow sharing of programs among users.

Let us consider a typical computer instruction, "clear A." This instruction, when translated into its unique number

("50AAAA") and executed by a central processor causes the location with address "AAAA" to be set to zero. (For our purposes here, we will use "AAAA" to represent the address: in an actual program, the address would be represented numerically.) The numerical representation has to tell the central processor at least two things: what to do (place "0" into a location), and what location to modify; that is, the numerical representation of the instruction must describe the operation to be performed and the address of a single operand. The digit "5" in the numerical representation for our instruction is called an *op code* (short for *operation code*) and when interpreted by the central processor it indicates what action has to be taken. The four digits represented by AAAA (with numbers substituted for letters in any actual case) give the address that we are dealing with. The "0" in the instruction also gives some information to the central processor, which we will deal with later in this chapter.

The "clear" instruction is an example of a one-address instruction, that is, enough information is given to find one address. An example of an instruction that has no address would be the "halt" instruction. We shall also consider examples of instructions that contain two addresses.

We describe the address to be cleared, in our hypothetical instruction, by putting the actual address into the instruction. This is known as *direct addressing*, and it is one of several possible "modes" of addressing. Another possible mode is *relative addressing*. In this mode, the instruction gives the location of the address to be cleared by stating its location relative to the instruction, rather than by stating its actual location

DIRECT ADDRESSING
10001000020

(Before)	10:	100
	20:	200
(After)	10:	100
	20:	100

FIGURE 5-1.

	1000:	11001010020
(Before)	1010:	100
	1020:	200

	1000:	11001010020
(After)	1010:	100
	1020:	100

FIGURE 5-2.

number. For instance, if the address of the "clear A" instruction were 347, a relative address of —4 would cause location 343 to be cleared; a relative address of +6 would cause location 353 to be cleared.

We may inquire as to how the central processor can properly interpret the instruction. Although the op code (5) is unambiguous, how can it tell whether the four digits represented by AAAA are a direct address or a relative address? This is where the "0" in our hypothetical instruction (50 AAAA) plays a part. If that 0 were changed to a 1, it could indicate that the rest of the instruction was to be treated as a relative address rather than an absolute address. Thus, the instruction "500010" could indicate that location 10 was to be cleared (the 0 indicates direct addressing). Similarly, the instruction "510010" could indicate that a location ten words beyond the location of the instruction was to be cleared (the 1 would indicate relative addressing). Our hypothetical instruction, therefore, contains three pieces of information: one is an op code, the second is the mode of addressing, and the third is the data needed to find the actual address.

There are a number of possible modes of addressing, of which we have considered two. A third mode is *indirect addressing*. The address coded in the instruction might not be the actual location to be cleared, but that address might contain the address of the location to be cleared. The indirect mode of addressing might be coded as "mode two." To take a concrete example, consider the instruction "520010." The 5

63

would indicate a "clear" operation. The 2 would indicate indirect addressing. Let us say that location 10 contains the number 100. In that case, execution of the instruction would cause location 100 to be cleared. If location 10 contained the number 200, then location 200 would be cleared.

Let us consider an instruction that moves a number from one place to another within memory. The instruction, "move A,B" might be coded "10AAAA0BBBB." The 1 would indicate that the operation to be performed is a move. AAAA and BBBB represent the numerical data necessary to calculate two addresses. The two 0s in this example would indicate direct addressing. Thus, the instruction "10001000020" would move the contents of location 10 to location 20, thus destroying whatever was previously in location 20. This is an example of a two-address instruction.

Consider the instruction "11001010020." We see that the move operation is again called for, and that both operands are addressed in relative mode. The first operand is ten words beyond the instruction and the second operand is twenty words beyond the instruction. Let us suppose this instruction is at location 1,000: its execution would cause the contents of location 1,010 to move to location 1,020. It is possible to have

INDIRECT ADDRESSING
12001020020

(Before)	10:	100
	20:	200
	100:	1776
	200:	105
(After)	10:	100
	20:	200
	100:	1776
	200:	1776

FIGURE 5-3.

64

20:	100	
100:	1776	
(Before)	1000:	11001020020
1010:	105	

20:	100	
100:	105	
(After)	1000:	11001020020
1010:	105	

FIGURE 5-4.

mixed addressing modes within an individual instruction. Take, for example, the instruction "10001020020." The mode for the first address is direct, and the mode for the second address is indirect. Hence we are going to find the number we want to move directly in location 10; but where shall we move it? To find the address to which we should move the number, we must look in location 20 where we might find, for example, the number 100. Address 100, therefore, is our destination. The number in location 10 would be moved to location 100, destroying whatever was in location 100.

This mixed mode example illustrates a general case for computer instructions. Each address within an instruction is specified by its own mode, and there is no reason why the modes of address for two or more addresses within an instruction need be the same. In fact, those examples where the modes of address for two or more instructions are the same probably illustrate an uncommon situation in computer programs.

Another useful mode of addressing is *immediate addressing.* With immediate addressing, the number we are interested in is actually in the instruction being executed. For example, assuming immediate addressing is "mode three," the instruction "13001000020" would move the number 10 into location 20 directly. Location 10 is unaffected and the previous contents of location 20 will be destroyed.

65

IMMEDIATE ADDRESSING
13001000020

(Before)	20:	105
(After)	20:	10

FIGURE 5-5.

Direct, indirect, relative, and immediate addressing are only four possibilities from a veritable galaxy. Virtually every computer has its own unique addressing modes, some more obscure than others.

Complicated instructions can contain many digits. For example, the "move" instruction we have invented contains eleven digits. If each is to be interpreted as an octal digit, the instruction will be thirty-three bits long. Execution time for an instruction includes the time it takes to fetch it from the memory. In any computer, long instructions (those with a lot of bits) take a longer time to be fetched from the memory, and their execution time is slower. Hence, it is not unreasonable for us to look for ways to shorten the number of bits in an instruction and thus effectively decrease its execution time.

Six bits (two octal digits) of the "move" instruction are used to indicate the addressing modes. If our imaginary computer had only one addressing mode, no bits would be necessary to specify it, for there would be no choice. On the other hand, a complicated job may require more than one instruction in a simple instruction set, and the execution of several simple instructions would take, potentially, more time than the execution of a single complex instruction. There is clearly no "correct" answer to this tradeoff.

If we do not wish to reduce the number of addressing modes in the computer in order to shorten instructions, there are still some tricks we can play. It is possible, for example, that we could reduce the number of digits we devote to the addresses in each instruction. In the examples shown, we have four digits for each address. There would be some savings if this were reduced to three. With three digits rather than four, however, we reduce the number of words that we can address in the memory. We can address locations 0 through 9999 with four digits but only locations 0 through 999 with three digits. Therefore, reducing the number of bits we assign for addresses is not a very good idea. Another possibility would be to try to eliminate one address entirely.

The solution of eliminating one address would seem to be absurd, because some instructions, such as the "clear," require an address in order to operate. In addition, the "move" instruction requires two addresses. What if, however, one of the addresses in each instruction were "assumed" to be a particular location? Since only one location would be possible, due to the design of the computer, it would not be necessary to specify that location in the instruction. To take a concrete example, let's assume that for a particular computer the special location is location 0. We would replace the "move" instruction we have described by two other instructions. One instruction moves any location to location 0 and the other moves location 0 to any location. In order to move from one arbitrary place to another both of these instructions would have to be executed. Each instruction would require the specification of only one address, since the other address for the "move" operation is assumed to be 0. It is not clear whether it takes more time to execute two simple instructions than one complicated one, so the usefulness of this tradeoff depends on the specific machine. What would we do with the "clear" instruction in a machine that assumes that one address is 0? If the "clear" instruction could clear only location 0, how could we clear an arbitrary location in the memory? We could clear location 0, and then move location 0 to an arbitrary location.

Computers with this sort of instruction set may be called *accumulator oriented*. In general, an arbitrary location in the memory is not chosen to have a special position in the instruction set. Rather, an extra register, called an *accumulator*, is placed in the central processor, and instructions always use the accumulator for one of their addresses. (See Figure 5-6.)

Because there may be only one accumulator in accumulator-oriented machines, in contrast to thousands of locations in the memory, it is possible to make the accumulator out of electronic materials that are considerably faster than locations in the memory. Thus, instructions that move the contents of an arbitrary memory location to the accumulator are faster than instructions that move the contents of an arbitrary location to another arbitrary location. There are two reasons for this: one we have already mentioned, namely, that an instruction with

Accumulator Oriented Instructions		General Register Oriented Instructions	
CLA 100000	CLEAR ACCUMULATOR	MOV	10AAAA0BBBB MOVE LOC A TO LOC B
LAC 20AAAA	LOAD ACCUMULATOR, MODE O, DIRECT ADDRESS	CLR	50AAAA CLEAR LOC A
DAC 30AAAA	STORE ACCUMULATOR, MODE O, DIRECT ADDRESS		

FIGURE 5-6. *Comparative programs.*

one assumed address has fewer bits that need to be fetched from the memory for execution than does an instruction with two addresses; the second is that one of the two locations involved is a very fast memory.

Whether we gain anything by adding an accumulator to our system depends on the characteristics of the individual machine. However, perhaps we could increase our gains by having more than one accumulator. We call computers with several accumulators *general purpose registers*. In some cases these registers can be treated exactly like locations in the memory, except that they are much faster, so instructions that use them are executed at a higher speed. In such cases, the general registers are usually given addresses that are small numbers, say 0 through 7. Because the addresses are small numbers, it takes very few bits to specify them. Hence, instructions specifying only these registers do not have to be very long, so they can be fetched at a relatively high speed by the central processor.

SUBROUTINES

If we know the instruction set of the computer we are using, we can write a program, translate it into numbers, and place the list of instructions comprising the program into the memory. We have assumed that this list of instructions was contiguous. That is, if a program were 100 words long, we would start somewhere and end 100 words later. It is not necessary, however, for the 100 instructions of a program to be in contiguous locations in the memory. We could put the first 50 in one place and the second 50 in some other place—for example, we could put the first 50 between locations 50 and 100 and the next 50 between locations 1,000 and 1,050. However, it would be necessary for us to put a "jump" instruction at the end of the first section so that the central processor would continue with the second section at the right place.

Consider a program that starts at "S" and ends at "E" and that does a number of things, among which it controls the Teletype to type the word "refrigerator" as a message to the user. The code to type the word "refrigerator" will be denoted by "squiggle," and in our hypothetical program "squiggle" might appear five times in five different places (see Figure 5-7). If the instructions necessary to type the word "refrig-

FIGURE 5-7. A program beginning at S and ending at E may contain within it the same group of instructions repeated several times.

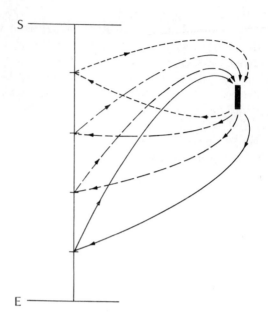

FIGURE 5-8. *We may avoid repetition of a group of instructions by reusing a single "copy" whenever we need it. This copy is called a* subroutine.

erator" require, say, 50 instructions, in order to accomplish the job five times we would have to place 250 instructions in the memory of the computer. This seems rather wasteful, because these 250 instructions will be the same 50 instructions repeated five times.

An alternative would be to have the code, "squiggle," in the memory only one time. Every time we need to do the function that "squiggle" represents, the main program would jump to "squiggle," "squiggle" would be executed, and then another jump would be made to return to the main program (see Figure 5-8). Each time "squiggle" was called we would have to execute two additional instructions: "jump" to it, and "return." For this example, the program would require additional instructions, and although these take time to execute, we would save 194 words in the memory by having "squiggle" represented only one time.

There is a difficulty, however, when we try to decide what instructions to use to make the various jumps. Since "squiggle" would be at known locations in the memory, all the jumps to "squiggle" from the main program are straightforward. The "jump" instruction introduced with DC-2 could be used, for example. A special "jump" instruction would be needed in order to return to the main program from "squiggle"; such an instruction would have to return to five different places on different occasions. One kind of "jump" instruction puts a new number in the program counter and also saves the number that it replaces in the program counter. This is entirely analogous to the operations performed when an external device interrupts the central processor. Routines that are called over and over again from a main program are known as *subroutines*. Our new kind of jump, which will be called a "subroutine jump," has two functions: it causes the central processor to begin fetching instructions from a new place in the memory, and it saves the old location from which instructions had been fetched. The old location, or program counter value, can be saved in a number of places; for instance, in special registers in the central processor or in location 0. The "subroutine return" instruction retrieves the old program counter value from its resting place and replaces it in the program counter, thus resuming execution of the main program. If we use the "subroutine jump" to jump to "squiggle," and if the last instruction executed in "squiggle" is a "subroutine return," we can use the "squiggle" code over and over again from the main program.

Can a subroutine call a subroutine? For example, can our subroutine to type the word "refrigerator" call a subroutine to type the letter "r," or the letter "e"? Of course it can. We encounter a problem, however, when we attempt to store the addresses to which we must return. If they are stored in a specific location, either in the memory or in special registers in the central processor, each additional subroutine "call" will not only store a return address but destroy the previous return address. This problem is analogous to that mentioned with interrupts of interrupts, and it is too complex to go into here.

Subroutines that type specific letters are obviously of limited use. It would be better if each time we called the subroutine we could tell it, in some way, what letter to type. The subroutine, due to its internal structure (a particular series of instructions) is able to do a general task such as typing a character; the main program makes available to the subroutine a number representing the particular character to be typed. The number made available to the subroutine is called a *parameter*:

the process is known as *passing parameters*. One way to pass parameters would be to put the parameter into a specific location in the memory, arbitrarily chosen; we would arbitrarily decide that the code for the character to be typed should go into location 1,000. Therefore, when the main program wanted to have a character typed, it would do the following: it would put the numerical code for the character into location 1,000, then it would call the subroutine by using the "subroutine jump." The subroutine would take the number in location 1,000 (whatever it might be) and cause it to be typed on the Teletype. It would then return to the main program by executing a "subroutine return."

Suppose that you forgot to include instructions in your program to place the numerical value of a character into the arbitrarily chosen location, in this case location 1,000. When the subroutine attempted to execute, it would retrieve from location 1,000 whatever number was there, perhaps an obscure number not representing any character. The Teletype would receive this obscure number and might type the wrong character or no character at all.

The use of subroutines is one of the most important organizational devices in program development. It is possible for you to write a subroutine to do a general purpose job, and then use it for years. It is not even necessary to remember how the subroutine works, only how to call it and how to pass parameters to it. In fact, you can use a subroutine written by other people if they tell you how it receives parameters, what it does, how it should be called and how it returns. Since subroutines can call other subroutines, it is possible to begin program development by writing a collection of simple subroutines, combining these into more complicated ones, and thus to build up a hierarchical program structure. When you are finished, the main program might be so simple that it does little more than call one or two complicated subroutines; these in turn would call simpler ones, and so on.

6

HOW CAN WE
USE COMPUTERS
EASILY?

The procedure for using virtually any computer currently available should now be quite clear. First, you must learn the instruction set. Then you decide on the problem you want to solve and write an appropriate program using the instruction set of the computer that you plan to use. This program must be translated from mnemonics that describe the instructions and are useful to the programmer into numbers that the central processor can understand. (*Mnemonics* are the letter abbreviations for instructions; for example, "GT" for "go to," or "CLR" for "clear.") The numbers must then be placed in the memory of the computer, and the program can be started. The difficulty is that translating mnemonics into numbers and loading numbers into a computer memory are time-consuming and tedious tasks that are prone to error. Hence, various methods have been developed to make the process of program development easier and less liable to error.

We should consider in detail the steps needed to implement a program, so that we can decide where the improvement can be made. The first step is thinking of a solution to the specific problem and writing that solution in the instruction set of the machine. This is the most difficult step, and we will discuss "user aids" later in this chapter. The second thing to be done is to translate the program, written in the instruction set of the computer, into a set of numbers. This process is not difficult but it is tedious. The next step in our process, loading the numbers into the memory, is also rather boring. The final step, starting the program, is easy. So it would appear that the places where we could get rid of tedious jobs would be in translating our program into numbers and in loading the numbers into the computer. Since both of these processes are well defined, there is no reason why we cannot write computer programs to help us with them. That is, we will write computer programs to help us to write computer programs.

Ideally, a computer program would read a program written on paper and translate that program into a set of numbers, which would also be placed on paper. A second program would then read the numbers on the paper and load them into the memory. Unfortunately, computers cannot read from paper with any dexterity, so we need another medium of exchange.

Computers can readily read and write paper tape—that is, they can read the holes in punched paper tape, and they can punch holes in paper tape. Any program that uses mnemonics for the instructions consists of a string of characters. Each character has a standard numerical representation, and these numbers can be punched in paper tape. Therefore, we can punch a program into paper tape. A program called an *editor* transfers our characters from the Teletype to paper tape. (See Figure 6-1.) Another program, called an *assembler*, can read that paper tape and translate the program into the appropriate numerical representations for the instructions. These numbers, in turn, can be punched into paper tape. Finally, when it comes time to load the program into the computer memory, a program called a *loader* can read the paper tape containing the numerical representation of the instructions, and can place the numbers into a list in the memory. The only task left would be to start and run the program.

This discussion of the use of an editor, assembler, and loader leaves a number of questions unanswered. First, where do these programs come from? Although, in principle, they could be written by the user of the computer, in fact they are usually supplied by the computer manufacturer. Each of these pro-

PROGRAM ON TELETYPE

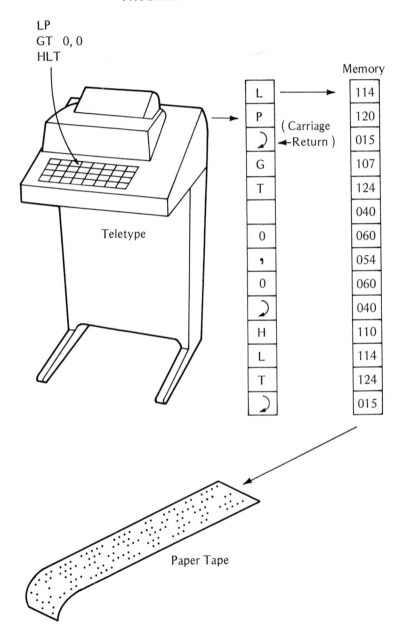

FIGURE 6-1. *The characters that we type on a Teletype are really represented in memory as a list of numbers, and these numbers may be transferred to holes in paper.*

grams may be several thousand instructions long, and if each person had to produce his own, it would be a big job. Second, if loading long programs into the memory is tedious and prone to error, how would we get these programs into the memory so that we could run them? If the loader were in the memory, it would be run in order to load the editor and the assembler from paper tape; but how would we get the loader into the memory? One way would be to write a loader that is very short—five or ten instructions long, for example. This could easily be placed in the computer memory by hand and run in order to load the assembler and the editor. Perhaps we should have two loaders—a small "bootstrap" loader, as they are called, and the main loader. The bootstrap loader will do nothing more than load the main loader, and the main loader will then load other programs such as the assembler and the editor, not to mention programs written by users. (See Figure 6-2.)

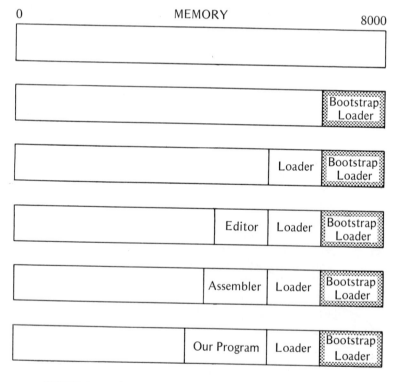

FIGURE 6-2. *This sequence of "memory maps" shows the sequence of programs located in memory and used in order to prepare a program.*

Let us review the procedure we would now use for program preparation and execution. First, we would load, by hand, the bootstrap loader into the memory of the computer—it is a short program. This program would be run in order to read the main loader from paper tape, and so the main loader would be placed in the memory. We would then run the main loader so as to read the editor from paper tape and place it in the memory, and we would start the editor. The editor would wait while we typed characters at the Teletype, and, among other things, it would punch these characters into paper tape. When we were finished, we would have a paper tape that contained our program with each instruction represented by its mnemonic in characters. We would again run the main loader in order to read the assembler, and the assembler would be read into the memory, thus destroying the editor. We could then run the assembler so that it would read the paper tape containing the character representation of our program and punch a new paper tape that would contain the numerical representation of our program. Next, we would run the main loader and read into the memory the numerical representation of our program, thus destroying the assembler. Finally, we could run our own program, which would now be in the memory.

The purpose of the editor is to transfer our program on a letter-by-letter basis into a form that can be read by a computer. We have assumed that it would transfer onto a punched paper tape a message that we type at the keyboard attached to a computer. However, paper tape is not the only medium on which an editor could put a message. It could place it on magnetic tape, punched cards, a disc, or the like. In fact, it could put it any place that numbers can be stored. Nevertheless, we will continue to use paper tape as our working example.

One way that the editor could work would be to wait for us to type a character at the keyboard. When we did so, it would immediately take the number produced from the keyboard and transfer it to paper tape, thus punching a set of holes into the paper. The process of punching holes, of course, is quite irreversible—if we make a mistake and type the wrong character, it will be immediately punched into the paper tape, and our tape will be incorrect. If we use the editor to prepare something other than a program—say, an essay—the misspelling of a single word would not be disastrous. However, in the computer program every instruction must be precisely correct, and if one instruction is misspelled, the entire program probably would not work. Therefore, an editor that punches our characters directly into paper tape would leave something to be desired. As a result, most editors do not punch holes directly into paper tape (or store the characters on any other medium) as we type characters at the keyboard. Rather, the editors store the characters, in numerical form, in a space allocated in the memory of the computer; this space is known as a *buffer*. When that space is filled, all of the characters are punched into paper tape. Since the memory of a computer can be read, it is possible, in principle, for us to go back and change some of the numbers in the memory, thus changing characters that we have mistyped. Editors usually contain provisions for doing this.

One common scheme is as follows: if you type the wrong character, immediately type a special character and the mistake will be "erased." Suppose that for a particular editor the special character is a "$." In that case, if you wish to type the word "move" and, in fact, have typed the word "mova," you could erase the last character by immediately typing a "$" and then typing an "e" to complete the word. This facility for erasing the last character can be extended in some editors so that if you type "$$$$," you would erase the previous four characters. Unfortunately, you will see at your Teletype the incorrectly spelled word, the character you have typed to erase the incorrect letter, and your letters for correction ("mova$e," for example).

Suppose that you were typing a line that was being received by the editor, and you discovered that you made a mistake at the beginning of the line and have typed twenty or thirty characters beyond. One thing you could do would be to strike the "$" twenty or thirty times in order to erase all of the characters back to the mistake. You could then continue to type the line. This is clearly a tedious procedure, and you might find that there is not enough space on the line to type all of the "$"s that you require. Hence, some editors have a second special character that will erase an entire line. Let us assume that this character is an "!" for a particular editor. If you type thirty or forty characters on a line and find that you do not wish to keep them, you need only type the "!" and the line will disappear from the memory, never to be seen again.

After you have completed typing your program you may

wish to save it on paper tape. In some way, the editor must be aware of your intentions, so many editors have a third special character, one that tells them you are finished inserting characters into the buffer. Let's assume that the special character is the "#." When you finished typing your program, you would end the last line with a carriage return, and then type a "#." The editor, upon seeing this special character, would punch into paper tape all the characters in your buffer. If, during the running of the editor, the buffer became filled, the editor might automatically enter the buffer onto paper tape and continue receiving characters from the keyboard.

To use the simple editor that I have described, you would indicate to the computer the address of the first word of the editor program, using the switches, buttons, and lights on the front of the computer. You would then press the starter switch, and the editor would be in motion. Most editors, when they begin, type a short message on the computer's printer so that the user knows that it is working properly. At this point you could begin typing your program, using the character-delete special character, and the line-delete special character as often as you wished. When you finished you would simply type the "#" (or its equivalent) and your program would be permanently saved. At this point your program would be in a form suitable for conversion to numerical representation by the assembler.

The capabilities of most editors go far beyond those that we have described. For example, consider a program that you have written and that you now wish to modify. It is on paper tape, irrevocably punched, and you want to create a new program that is exactly the same with the exception of one or two instructions. Such changes are often necessary because you find that the program you have originally written does not do exactly what you wish. One solution would be to run the editor as previously described and retype the whole program, making the few changes that are necessary; but this is rather wasteful. For that reason, editors also have the capability of reading paper tape representations of programs (or any other character string, such as essays, stories, or the like) into the computer memory, allowing the user to make modifications, and producing a new paper tape. An editor that does this will read the characters from the original paper tape into a buffer in the memory, and then allow the user to type various commands, telling the editor what changes to make. The paper tape to be corrected will not be listed on the Teletype unless the user makes a special request to the editor.

You may ask how an editor will know, once it is started, whether you wish to create a new program by inputting characters at the keyboard, or whether you wish to modify an old program by reading it in from paper tape. One way would be to type a special character as a signal to the editor, once it had started, that would tell it which function the user wanted. For example, you could type the letter "i" to indicate the input of a new program, or the letter "e" to indicate the editing of an old program. If you typed the letter "e," it would be your responsibility to place a paper tape in the paper tape reader so that the editor could read it.

Editors differ greatly in the variety of commands that they can handle for modifying programs or text. Some editors are strictly line-oriented. That is, commands typed by the user indicate a line, by number, and the editor can delete or insert individual lines. Suppose, for example, that a program contains 100 lines. It would be possible to lengthen the program by adding lines following line 100, or to delete any given line by indicating its number. And it would be possible to insert lines somewhere in the middle of the program following a specific numbered line.

Some editors, in contrast, are context-oriented. They allow the user to search for a specific string of characters in the buffer, and to change that string to anything else. The string may be as short as a single character, or may be as long as several lines. For example, suppose that one wished to change, in a buffer, all instructions labeled "lp" to an instruction labeled "dp." A command could be typed at the keyboard that would cause the editor to search for every occurrence of the character pair "lp" and substitute for it the character pair "dp." One could so modify only the first occurrence of the pair "lp" or, for that matter, the tenth occurrence, the fifteenth occurrence, or whatever one wished. This context-oriented facility is a very powerful one, and allows the user to easily modify his programs or text. A special character would have to be typed into the editor when the editing process was finished, so that the editor could save the new, modified, character string on a storage medium such as paper tape.

The assembler is a program that reads a paper tape containing a program represented by a string of characters and produces a paper tape containing a list of numbers—the numerical representations of the instructions. The latter can be interpreted by the central processor of the computer so the program can be executed. As with the editor, media other than paper tape can be used for storage. However, we will continue to use paper tape for our example. The assembler program is read into the memory of the computer by a loader, and the starting address is indicated by the user. A typical assembler will type a message on the keyboard to let the user know that it is working properly, and it will then proceed to read the paper tape with the character representation of the program.

Assemblers perform a variety of tasks; for instance, they can detect errors. If you mistype an instruction and do not correct your error in the editor, the assembler will be put in the position of trying to convert an instruction of which it is totally ignorant. It will refuse to produce a paper tape containing a set of numbers and will type a message—an "error" message—to the user. Hopefully, this "error" message will give enough information so that the user can find the error in his program and can correct it by using the editor.

Assuming that the program was typed in a form that is acceptable to the assembler, the assembler could convert the instructions into numbers. The description of the format to be followed is supplied by the manufacturer. Typically, a program would consist of a series of lines and each line would contain one instruction. This is exactly the way we have written programs for DC-1 and DC-2. Each line, moreover, is divided into a number of parts. You will remember that the line with instructions for DC-1 and DC-2 could be divided into two parts: one part was a description of the instruction to be followed (the "op" code), and the second part was the list of operands for that instruction, separated by commas. For example, the "go to" instruction would be written "gt x,y." The "gt" tells the assembler what "op" code to translate, and the "x,y" tells the assembler what numbers to place in the rest of the instruction word. To take a second example, the "jump" instruction would be written "jmp 1,000," "jmp 1," or the like.

Let us assume that we are writing a program one or two thousand words long. If, somewhere in the program, we wish to write a "jump" instruction to some other place, it is necessary for us to know the address of the other place. We could find this address, in principle, by counting instructions from the top of the program, but we may have to count for a long time. In addition, some instructions are two or more words long in the memory, but are written on one line when writing a program. In our counting, we would have to keep watch for such instructions and correct our counting procedure accordingly. Such a counting procedure would be time consuming, tedious, and prone to error. In addition, if there were a number of "jump" instructions in a program, the difficulty of the task would be multiplied manifold. Since the counting process is, however, quite simple, it is reasonable to inquire whether assemblers can do the job for us, and of course they can. The method employed is to add a third piece of information to some instruction lines. This third piece of information is a symbolic name, in characters, for that line. For example, the instruction "go to 10,20" could be named "top" and the line would be written as shown in Figure 6-3. The user can choose

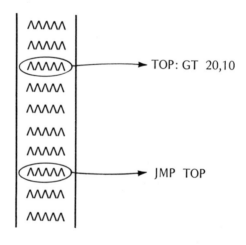

FIGURE 6-3. *Instructions in programs may be given symbolic names that can then be used by other instructions in the program.*

any name that he wishes for an individual instruction, within a few limits, and can name as many or as few instructions as he wishes. The important point is that the symbolic name for an instruction can then be referred to by other instructions. For example, if, later in the program, the user required an instruction that jumped to the "go to 10,20" instruction, he could simply write "jmp top."

Assemblers with a symbolic-name facility work in at least two stages. In the first stage they go through the entire program looking for symbolic names. They count as they go along, and they create a table, in the memory, of symbolic names and the associated addresses. This table contains, of course, nothing but numbers in a particular format—the characters comprising the symbolic name are represented by numbers. On a second "pass" through the program, the assembler would make the actual conversions of instructions into numbers and would refer to the symbolic name table, with address assignments, whenever it needed that information. If you name a location but then never refer to it by name with another instruction, no harm is done. However, if you forget to name an instruction, and then do refer to it by name in another instruction, the assembler is at a loss—it does not know to what instruction you are referring, and it will produce an "error message."

We have tacitly assumed that the program you present to the assembler can have only two kinds of lines—lines containing acceptable instructions in proper formats, and lines that are mistakes. Actually, a third kind of line can be included in your program, and such lines may be called *assembler-directives*. These are special code words that direct the assembler to do something other than convert instructions into numerical form. Assembler directives do not produce instructions, rather, they are commands to the assembler. To take a trivial example, suppose that an assembler in use not only produces a set of numbers but also prints that list of numbers on a printer for reference by the user. One assembler directive might be the code word "page." Whenever the assembler, during its conversion, comes to a line containing the word "page," it will skip a page on the printer. This will allow the user to have a more readable list of numbers because he can divide it into logical pages. Most assemblers interpret a variety of assembler directives, some of which are considerably more useful than the one presented.

Imagine a program that does a number of things, one of which is repeated four or five times. Thus, several instructions, in a given sequence, will occur in this program in a number of places. We encountered this example before when we discussed subroutines. The solution presented at that time was to define the short sequence of instructions forming the repeated function as a subroutine, and then at each point where its action was required, to jump to that subroutine by using a special "subroutine jump" instruction. The subroutine, in turn, would return to the main program by using a "subroutine return" instruction. This solution saves space in that the instructions need be represented only once. However, it slows the execution of the program, because a "subroutine jump" and a "subroutine return" must be executed in addition to the repeated instructions whenever their action is desired. If a slowly running program is intolerable, and if sufficient memory space is available for repeating the sets of instructions, it may be advisable to abandon this subroutine solution. We are then left with the problem of typing this list of instructions over and over again, while entering our main program into an editor. Assemblers with a *macro* capability can help us in this task. A macro is a list of instructions that can be made equivalent to a single key word. The user can define a macro at the beginning of his program, and whenever this key word is written into the program by the user, the assembler will automatically place, at that location in the program, the instructions as previously defined. Ten or twenty instructions, for example, could be represented by a single word. The instructions necessary to draw a square could all be made equivalent to the word "square," and whenever we wished to draw a square, we would simply include a line in our program with the word "square." This capability is akin to the assembler directive, in that the code words defined as macros do not produce single instructions. In contrast to assembler directives that produce no instructions, macros produce a large number of instructions.

In order to make use of the macro facility, we must have a way of defining macros at the beginning of our programs. To this end, a typical assembler would have two directives: one to start the definition of a macro, and one to end it. The first directive would be followed by the lines of instructions that form the content of the macro. The last such instruction would be followed by an assembler directive that ends the definition of that macro. Several macro definitions could be included at the beginning of the program. When the assembler reads these macro definitions, it produces no instructions. However, it does remember the definition of each macro so that later it can make the proper substitutions when key words appear in the main program.

Let us consider in some detail the example shown in Figure 6-4. The assembler reads a paper tape that contains a number

of characters. The characters begin "d e f m a c s q" and end
with the characters "h l t (return)." The assembler produces
instructions beginning at the point indicated by the start of
the main program and ending with the "halt" instruction. At
the beginning of the tape, however, is a macro definition. The
assembler directive to begin the definition of a macro is
"defmac" and the assembler directive to end the definition is
"endmac." The "defmac" assembler directive is somewhat
complicated, in that the line containing the assembler directive must also contain the name of the macro, in this case

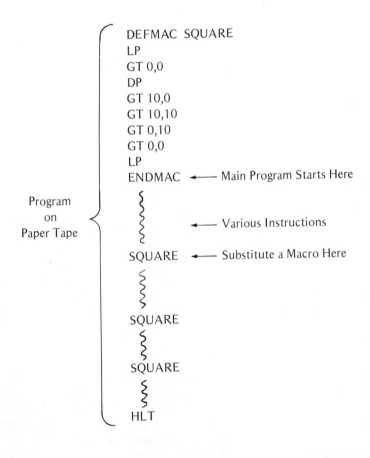

FIGURE 6-4. *By defining macros (lists of instructions that are
given a single name) it is possible to reduce the number of lines
of instructions that we must prepare.*

85

"square." If we named a macro "cucumber," the line would be "defmac cucumber." After the beginning of the macro definition, the actual instructions comprising the macro are listed. Remember, however, that the assembler produces no instruction numbers when it sees these macro definition lines. At the start of the main program, the assembler begins to translate instructions into numbers. When it reaches a line containing the word "square," it substitutes for that line the eight lines of instructions in the macro definition, translating those eight lines into numbers. It then continues, substituting the macro definition every time the word "square" is encountered. Like the editor, the assembler searches for a character string and substitutes for it another character string.

An assembler with a macro definition as described would not be particularly powerful. In the case shown, for example, every time the macro "square" is invoked, a square with sides of length 10 would be drawn. It would be much better if there were some way to draw a square of any arbitrary size. With a subroutine, this would be easy. We would simply pass the length of the side, as the parameter, to the subroutine. The macro capabilities of some assemblers allow a process that is a limited form of passing of parameters. The user simply gives a symbolic name, in the macro definition, to one or more parameters. Then, when invoking the macro, the user indicates an actual number to be substituted for the symbolic name. For example, we may define a macro "square" with a parameter arbitrarily called "a." The macro definition includes a number of instructions referring to a quantity—"a." Of course, since "a" is unknown at this point, no instructions could be generated. At each point that "square" is to be invoked, the macro must be "called" with the parameter value indicated. This is done in two cases in Figure 6-5—"square 10" and "square 15." At the first instance, instructions will be generated that substitute the number 10 for every occurrence of the symbol "a," thus generating instructions to draw a square with side 10. At the second instance, the number 15 will be substituted for every occurrence of the symbol "a" and so instructions to draw a square with side 15 will be generated. Notice that the process of string substitution is repeated here. The string "15" is substituted for the string "a," and new, definite instructions are created. The assembler proper, in turn, can convert these instructions into numerical representations.

It is important to realize that a macro definition capability

DEFMAC SQUARE A

```
LP
GT 0,O
DP
GT A,O
GT A,A
GT O,A
GT O,O
LP
ENDMAC
  }
SQUARE  10
  }
  }
  }
  }
  }
  }
  }
SQUARE  15
  }
  }
  }
HLT
```

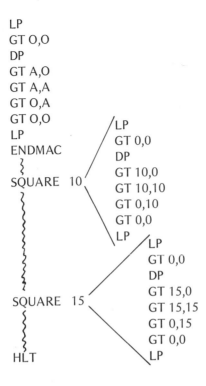

```
LP
GT 0,0
DP
GT 10,0
GT 10,10
GT 0,10
GT 0,0
LP
       LP
       GT 0,0
       DP
       GT 15,0
       GT 15,15
       GT 0,15
       GT 0,0
       LP
```

FIGURE 6-5. *A macro definition capability may allow the passing of parameters, similar to the way parameters can be passed to a subroutine.*

of this sort can be extremely powerful. At the beginning of our program tape, we can define a number of macros that represent functions that are important to our application. For example, a draftsman might define macros to draw various geometric shapes, or a mathematician might define macros to evaluate a number of functions. Our main program might contain a few lines of instructions and many lines of macros. Thus, most or all of the program would appear to contain instructions in a form useful for the application at hand. Each of our macro definitions would be expanded by the assembler into normal instructions—we would not have to do the job. You will remember that one of the most difficult aspects of program writing is converting a problem from everyday terms into a list of instructions understandable by the computer. If we can make up a set of powerful macro definitions, the translation process can be simplified. Then we need only to describe the solution to our problem in a set of standard terms that are especially tailored for the problem at hand. The assembler will have the difficult job of expanding each macro into a set of instructions. Note, however, it is still our responsibility to define the macros at the beginning of our program. Hence, the intellectual savings may be a figment of our imagination.

The intellectual savings would be very real, however, if we could use macros that had been previously defined by us or by others faced with a problem similar to ours. If someone else, for example, had a problem of a similar nature and defined a set of macros that could be combined into a program to easily solve that problem, perhaps we could use his macros. One possibility would be to combine his macros with our main program into a single paper tape. If problems of a given sort, requiring a given set of macros, were frequently encountered, it would be helpful if a set of macros could be permanently built into the assembler. The assemblers of some computers have sufficient flexibility so that this is possible, and we can tailor such assemblers to our particular kind of problem. The programs we write may contain few instructions in the instruction set of the machine, but may instead invoke a set of macros. The assembler will expand these macros into instructions that can be understood by the central processing unit, and will translate those instructions into numbers. The numbers can then be loaded by the loader and the program can be run. In effect, the language we would use to communicate with the computer would be closer to human language, and in particular to human language associated with particular kinds of problems, than the communication we have discussed to this point, namely, the individual instructions in the instruction set of the computer.

Since we can use macros produced by other people, and a set of macros can be more or less permanently attached to an assembler, we could keep several assemblers at our disposal. One assembler might have, for example, a set of macros associated with it for doing statistical calculations. Another assembler might have a set of macros for doing various household calculations, such as budgets, calories, or checkbooks. The manufacturer of the computer might supply, along with a regular assembler, a set of assemblers—each with a specialized collection of macros. Manufacturers do not, in fact, do this, but they do supply a number of programs, called *compilers*, with the computer. Compilers are not the same as assemblers with powerful macro capabilities, although their functions are very similar. They convert a character string representing our program into a list of numbers that contains instructions that the central processor of the computer can interpret and execute. The character string that represents our program consists of several lines of instructions in a language that is specific for a particular kind of problem. For example, a program that could be converted to instructions by a statistics compiler might be in a form that would be understandable to statisticians who are totally ignorant of computers.

Each compiler is built to interpret a limited subset of the language we use every day, and to interpret it only when it is presented in proper format. Since compilers are programs, just as assemblers are programs, the formats are defined by the original writer of that program and are described by the manufacturer of the computer.

The number of compilers currently available is huge. They are usually written in the instruction set of a particular computer. Hence, the number of compilers available for an individual computer may be limited. A typical computer might have one compiler for interpreting a language that describes algebraic problems, another for drawing complicated pictures, and perhaps a third for doing business calculations.

Compilers are used in a way that is very similar to assemblers. Since a compiler is a normal program, it can be loaded by a loader and started by the user. At this point, it reads a paper tape (to continue our paper tape examples), which contains a character string that is the program written by the user in the language that the compiler understands. The paper tape could be prepared by a sophisticated editor or by a hand paper tape punch—all that matters is that the holes are in the right places so that the characters describe commands in the language of the compiler at hand. After a while, the compiler will produce a paper tape containing a list of numbers that are instructions that can be executed by the central processor. The list of numbers can then be loaded by the loader, and the program the user has written can be run.

One type of compiler interprets a language called FORTRAN. FORTRAN compilers are exceedingly popular because FORTRAN is an easy language to learn and to use and because FORTRAN is available for a large number of different computers. FORTRAN is one of the oldest computer languages currently in use, and resistance to change has caused it to be passed from generation to generation of computer users. I have listed a few examples of short FORTRAN programs. None of these programs does anything very interesting. You will see, however, that if the types of commands in all of these examples were combined into one long FORTRAN program, it could be made to do something quite useful. A number of commands in the FORTRAN language will be excluded from this discussion. In particular, the commands that are used for getting information in and out of the memory and for controlling peripheral devices have been eliminated. One can, however, read about them in any manual that describes the FORTRAN language.

The first example (Figure 6-6) is input to the FORTRAN com-

I = 1

END

FIGURE 6-6.

piler that is two lines long and consists of the character string "I = 1 (return) E N D (return)." From these eight characters the compiler would produce a program, in numerical form, that might be as short as two instructions. The last of the two instructions might be a "halt" instruction. The first of the two instructions has a simple job—it must move a number from one place in the memory to another. The "equals" sign in the FORTRAN program implies that a "move" operation is called for, that is, a number will be copied from one location into another. The compiler will arbitrarily decide on two locations. It will place the number "1" into one of these locations. It will consider the other location to have the symbolic name "I." So, when we start the program the value "1" will be copied from one chosen location to another chosen location. After this, a "halt" instruction will be fetched and executed by the central processor.

The second example (Figure 6-7) is a little longer, and the

```
J = 1

I = J

END
```

FIGURE 6-7.

FORTRAN compiler will produce a series of computer instructions that will cause two moves to take place before the program halts. The first move will be between an arbitrary location containing the number "1" and another arbitrary location that is symbolically named "J." The second move will be from the location symbolically named "J" to the location symbolically named "I." Thus, when all is over, the location named "J" will contain a "1" and the location named "I" will contain a "1."

If all that one could accomplish in the FORTRAN language were to move numbers from place to place, it would not be terribly useful for solving problems. However, it is possible to do arithmetic in FORTRAN, as we shall see in our third example (Figure 6-8). The first instruction of this program will take

```
J = 1

I = J + J

END
```

FIGURE 6-8.

the number "1" from an arbitrary location and place it in another arbitrary location symbolically named "J." The second instruction, however, is somewhat more complicated. The contents of location "J" will be copied to a location in the memory chosen by the compiler. Then, the contents of location "J" will be added to the contents of the location in the memory chosen by the compiler, leaving the sum in that location. This sum will be transferred to location "I." Since "J" contains a 1 after the first instruction is executed, "J" + "J" is 2. Hence the number "2" will be moved by the second line of instruction to the arbitrarily chosen location "I." After this the program will halt. What would happen if the first instruction ("J = 1") were missing? Some compilers begin by initially placing "0" in all their symbolically named locations. Thus "J + J" would be 0, and the second instruction would move a "0" into "I." This is somewhat unnecessary, because "I" would also have been initially set to 0.

Our fourth example (Figure 6-9) demonstrates that arithme-

$$I = 1$$

$$J = I * I + I/I$$

END

FIGURE 6-9.

tic in FORTRAN is not limited to addition. In general, the * symbol is used to indicate multiplication and the / symbol is used to indicate division. Execution of the first instruction will move a number "1" from some location to another, named "I." The second line will be expanded by the compiler into a number of instructions that the central processor must execute. These instructions cause a multiplication to be accomplished as well as an addition. The multiplication of "I * I" leaves the numerical value of 1. So does the division of "I / I." The sum of the multiplication and division is 2. Hence, the number "2" will be placed in an arbitrarily chosen location named "J," at which point the program will halt. The programmer need write only one line of instruction ("J = I * I + I / I") in FORTRAN and it can be expanded by the compiler instructions.

Figure 6-10 demonstrates the FORTRAN equivalents of "jump" instructions and the symbolic naming of instruction lines. The first line in the program has been given the name

```
1     I = 1

      J = I + 1

      GO TO 1
```

FIGURE 6-10.

"1." The last line in the program is equivalent to a "jump" instruction that will cause the central processor to go back to "1." This program will never end. First, the number "1" will be moved from a location to another location named "I." Then, "I" will be added to "I" to produce a numerical value of 2, and the "2" will be moved to a location named "J" replacing the previous contents of "J." The "jump" instruction will then be executed, causing the whole procedure to be repeated.

Figure 6-11 demonstrates the "if" instruction. The first, sec-

```
1     J = −10

2     J = J + 1

      IF (J + J) 2,3,3

3     END
```

FIGURE 6-11.

ond, and fourth lines are familiar forms, and each is given a symbolic name—1, 2, or 3. The first line will cause a number to be moved from one location to another, named "J." The second line causes a number to be added to the contents of "J," and the results are placed back in location "J." After the first line is executed, "J" contains −10. After the second line is executed, "J" contains −9 (one more than −10). The "if" statement causes a calculation to be done and this calculation is included in the parentheses. We have chosen to calculate a quantity that is "J + J": we could just as easily calculate "J + 2," "J * J," or anything else. In this case, just before the "if" statement is executed, "J" contains −9; −9 + −9 is −18. The result is negative. The last part of the "if" statement is a list of three locations. If "J + J" turned out to be negative (as it was this time), the "if" statement would act as a "jump" to the line labeled 2. If "J + J" turned out to be 0, the "if" statement would act as a "jump" to the line labeled 3 (a halt). If "J + J" turned out to be positive, the "if" instruction would act as a "jump" to location 3. The "2, 3, 3," at the end of the "if" statement is arbitrary, depending on what we want the program to do. We could have written any three numbers there we wished, provided that each number was a statement name.

Let us think carefully about what this program will do. The first time we reach the "if" statement, "J" contains −9, "J + J" is negative, and so we will "jump" to the instruction labeled "2." At this point, 1 will be added to the contents of "J," leaving the result, −8, in "J." We will then go on to the "if" statement, and calculate "J + J." Since "J + J" is −16, we again "jump" to statement 2 and add 1 to "J." Adding 1 to "J" gives us −7, after which we proceed to the "if" statement and calculate "J + J" is −14. Since this is again negative, we return to statement 2. You can easily see that this little loop will continue for some time. "J" will go from −7 to −6 to −5, and so on until it reaches 0. When it does, "J + J" will no longer be negative, but will be 0. Hence, the "if" statement will act as a "jump" to the location labeled "3," which is, in this case, a "halt." We have set up a primitive counting operation. We were able to do something ten times, although what we did was not very useful. Obviously, however, we could do something considerably more useful any number of times that we wished.

The FORTRAN language allows you to control various peripheral devices, to define subroutines, to deal with lists of numbers in convenient ways, and to do complex arithmetic calculations. In addition, most FORTRAN compilers give you the capability of easily calculating common mathematical functions, such as trigonometric functions, exponential functions, logarithmic functions, and the like.

In all cases, the compiler translates a list of characters comprising a program into a list of numbers that are instructions that can be executed by the computer. There are a number of reasons for writing programs in this way:

1. Complicated things are more easily done with a language such as FORTRAN than with individual instructions in the instruction set of the machine you are using. Arithmetic calculations, for example, are greatly simplified by FORTRAN.

2. Programs written in FORTRAN, or in similar languages, are transferable from computer to computer. If you write a program in FORTRAN, it can just as easily be read by a compiler running on one computer as by a compiler running on another. There may be slight differences that would necessitate small editing changes, but such differences are rare. If you write a program in FORTRAN, or any other language for which a number of compilers are available, you need not worry about having to write new programs when you use a different computer. On the other hand, if you write your programs in the instruction set of the machine you are currently using, you will have to rewrite your program in the instruction set of a new machine if you make a switch.

So far in this chapter we have discussed several methods that people can use to facilitate the writing of computer programs. Aids such as editors, assemblers, macro assemblers, and compilers are of little use, however, if they cannot be easily loaded into the computer.

A simple loader will do little more than read a paper tape that contains a list of numbers and place these numbers into the memory of the computer. More complicated loaders, however, do exist. For example, consider a situation in which your program is in several pieces: you may have written one piece to type things on the printer, another piece to draw pictures with a plotter, another piece to do mathematical calculations, and so on. You now wish to combine all of these programs with a main program that will direct their operations. The loader will load each of the paper tapes, placing the programs in the proper locations in the memory so that they do not overlap and destroy each other.

The scheme that has been described for using editors, assemblers, compilers, and loaders involves a lot of paper tape. Since some of the programs we have to read are quite long (thousands of instructions), it will take some time to read them from paper tape, and there is always a chance of error due to ripping the paper tape, or the like. It would be desirable to avoid paper tape entirely and keep all of our programs on some other storage medium, such as magnetic tape or a disc. There is no easy way, however, to load the right program from a disc into the memory. With paper tape, we choose the program we want to read by manually selecting from a variety of paper tapes and placing the proper one in the paper tape reader. There is no parallel operation for the disc. We cannot manually stop the disc, rotate it until the program we want is underneath the magnetic reading and writing head, and then start spinning the disc.

If we cannot select the proper program on the disc manually, we will have to do it via program control. For this purpose, we use a relatively complex loader that will deal with the disc and the Teletype attached to the computer. When we type the name of the program that we want from the disc, the loader goes to the disc, finds that program, and loads it into the memory. We may ask how this complicated loader can find the program. To do so, a part of the disc is arbitrarily chosen to be a *directory*. The directory is a list containing, in numerical form, the names and locations of the programs on the disc. After we type the name of the program on the Teletype, we strike a carriage return and the loader compares the characters we have typed with each of the names in the directory of the disc. To do this, it must read all or part of the directory from the disc into the memory, and then make the comparison. When it finds a program with the same name that we have typed, it checks in the directory to see where that program is on the disc, and then reads it from the disc to the memory. If it does not find a program with the same name as we have typed, it will print an "error" message on the Teletype. How does the complicated loader know where to find the directory on the disc? An arbitrary place on the disc is defined as the directory location. This location is set up by the programmer who writes the original loader. Most commonly, such a complicated loader is supplied by the manufacturer, so the manufacturer of the computer decides where on the disc the directory is going to be located.

Although the scheme just outlined eliminates the need for separate paper tapes for editors, assemblers, and compilers, what about the paper tapes we have been using to contain our programs, both in character form and in numerical form? Would it not be possible for the editor, for example, to produce a list of characters on the disc rather than a list of characters punched in the paper tape? This is entirely possible: all that is necessary is for this list of characters, our program, to be given a name, and for the editor to enter this name into the directory on the disc. If we told the assembler the name of our program, it could find our program on the disc by consulting the directory. In turn, the assembler could produce a numerical representation of our program on the disc, and give this numerical representation a name that we have chosen. At this stage, we would have completely eliminated paper tape from our operations.

Since the loader, editors, assemblers, and compilers all have to be coordinated to use the same disc and the same directory, these programs are treated as a unified whole known as an *operating system*. What we have described above is a very primitive operating system.

More complicated operating systems can do a number of things for computer users. For example, operating systems contain routines and subroutines for reading and writing things on the disc. If the user attempted to read or write things on the disc independently of the operating system, he might inadvertently destroy the directory and programs on the disc. Therefore, computer manufacturers often provide programs that contain routines or subroutines for reading and writing things on the disc.

You do not need an operating system in order to use a computer. You can write a program using the instruction set of the machine, translate it into numbers, and enter those numbers into the computer by hand. Then you can start the program and, hopefully, it will run to completion. If that is too difficult, you can use an editor, an assembler, and a loader supplied by the manufacturer of the machine. If you use these programs, it will not be necessary for you to translate your instructions into numbers and to enter these numbers into the computer by hand. Your program will not run any better, but you will probably make fewer trivial mistakes. If the difficulties of loading the loader into the memory are too great, you can use an operating system. The use of the operating system gives you other advantages as well. Your programs can make use of subroutines in the operating system, thus saving you time in writing programs. In addition, operating systems frequently make heavy use of a disc, which is considerably faster than paper tape readers.

7

HOW CAN
PEOPLE SHARE
COMPUTERS?

Computers execute instructions very rapidly (programs that are of moderate length can be executed within a short amount of time—less than a second). Imagine yourself typing commands to the operating system, telling it to run various programs. Each program that you tell it to run will take a very short time to execute, and most of the time during this "interaction" will be spent by the operating system waiting for you to type new commands. The human factor will limit the speed of operation of the system. Although this is not always true, it is typically the case. We could inquire whether it would be possible to use the time that would otherwise be wasted waiting in some profitable way. For example, we could connect two Teletypes to a computer and have two people type commands to the operating system. While one of the two users was typing his command, the operating system could be executing a program for the other user. What would happen in case of conflict—what would happen if two people requested programs to be run at the same time? This is similar to a problem that was faced when we discussed interrupts in the computer. It is possible that two users could have different priorities, so one user would always be given preference; or the one who typed his command first could be given preference and the other would have to wait for a response. The person who had to wait would only have to wait for a short time and might not even notice the delay. What would happen if one of the two users commanded the operating system to run a program that took one or two hours to execute? Would the other user have to wait until it was finished? One way to avoid this problem would be to share equally the total time available. The computer would begin to run the very long program, but after a short time the operating system would stop the program in order to check the Teletype of the second user, to see if there were any commands outstanding. If there were, it might attempt to execute them in a short time before returning to the long program. The long program would take longer to finish because there was a second' user, but possibly not appreciably longer.

With this scheme we have a situation in which two people appear to use a computer independently of each other. The computer is actually allocating time between them, so that neither is unduly delayed, and both can get useful work done. The only problem is that programs executed by each user will operate at a lower speed than if there were only one user. There are several reasons for this reduction in speed. The obvious one is that the operating system is alternating between two programs, and so each one is getting only a fraction of the time. A less obvious reason is that the operating system must do some computation in order to decide when to interrupt one program and switch to another, and this computation takes time. Such calculations of the operating system are called *overhead*. If the amount of calculation the operating system must engage in (overhead) is large, then the amount of time left to execute programs requested by users may be small. Although they are inefficient, many such systems exist.

We have painted a picture of two users working with a single computer, but if a computer were fast enough, it could handle more than two users. Systems that do this are called *time-sharing systems*, and some time-sharing systems can give adequate service, apparently simultaneously, to many independent users. How many users can such a system service? The average for time-sharing systems currently in use is probably fifty to sixty. Some systems, however, can service several hundred users, and in the near future systems servicing thousands of users are not unlikely. There are several important points to remember. First, the users are not aware of each other and can work entirely independently. Second, although it may appear that they are working simultaneously, actually the computer is alternating among them, attending to each in turn. This results in a decrease in program execution speed for each user. Hence, you cannot use a time-sharing system if you want your programs to be executed at maximum speed.

We cannot expect programs that we run using a time-sharing system to run at a constant rate. A variable number of people will be using the system, and they will be randomly requesting service. Their requests for service are differentially demanding—ranging from trivial tasks to difficult jobs. Thus, the user of a time-sharing system is faced with a computer that is variable in its speed of service, but, nevertheless, easy to use.

If you use a time-sharing system, you may not believe that you are using a computer at all. Your only interaction with the computer will be through a Teletype, or similar typewriter-like device. As you will see in the next chapter, these Teletypes may be located at some distance from the main computer: you may never see the computer at all.

In order for a time-sharing system to work properly, the users must not be able to interfere with each other. This places some restrictions on what an individual user can do. For example, you cannot simply halt the computer in order to observe what numbers are in particular locations in the memory. Furthermore, you cannot type any possible commands to the operating system: it will accept only those commands that can be followed without harming other users. Despite your remote location from the computer and the restrictions on the programs you can run, time-sharing computers are very much like the computers that are for single users.

The pattern we might develop would be one of typing a command—waiting for its execution; typing a command—waiting for its execution; and so on. It is possible that we know exactly what we wish to do with a computer and have the list of commands we intend to type firmly in mind. In that case, it may be unnecessary for us to wait for each command to be executed before typing the next. To this end, some operating systems give us the capability of presenting a list of requests at one time. The operating system will examine each request in turn, and do what we wish. If all goes well, it can type a message to that effect when it has completed all of our commands. If, on the other hand, an error is developed somewhere during the process, it can also inform us of that fact. Systems that use this sort of organization may be called *batch operating systems*. In most cases, the user of a batch operating system must punch his commands into punched cards, one command per card. The stack of cards containing the list of commands can then be read by a card reader on the computer.

The most obvious advantage of a system of this sort is that the user need not wait for all of his commands to be finished: they can be entered into the computer, and the user can leave, returning later to see if his list of commands has been properly executed.

While the user is waiting for his commands to be completed, there is no reason why a second user cannot enter his own sequence of requests into the computer. These might be added to the list of things to be done and the computer could take them in turn. The computer could handle requests, in sequence, for a number of users. The difference between this batch system and the time-sharing system previously mentioned is mostly one of timing. The time between entering a request to a time-sharing operating system and receiving a response may be on the order of seconds. However, at any one time most batch operating systems have a long list of commands from users, and a newly-entered set of commands may take several hours to "come up." This delay is commonly called *turn-around time*.

It is not always true that batch operating systems execute the requests of users in the order in which they are received. One variation on this basic scheme would be to give individual users their own priority. Requests for service from users with higher priority might be pushed to the top of the list and receive faster service. How could the computer know what commands came from which user? If the commands of the operating system were to take the form of a stack of punched cards, the first card on this stack might contain some identification material for the particular user.

Another variation would be to execute the programs in an order that would keep the central processor and the peripherals of the computer maximally busy. For example, suppose one program required a great deal of printing. Rather than wait for the printing to be completed, the computer could begin to execute a second user's program. Because a printer is so slow, most of the central processor's attention could be devoted to this second program, with very few instructions needed to keep the printer operating at maximal speed. Carrying this idea a bit further, a number of modern batch computers keep several users' programs in the memory at one time. The operating system alternates among these programs in order to keep the central processor and the peripherals maximally busy. Such a system is called a *multiprogramming system.*

The possibilities that a user faces differ primarily in the amount of time that he has to wait in order to have programs executed. In order to obtain the fastest possible response, the user should have his own computer and only one person should use it at any one time. If small time delays are acceptable, a number of people can simultaneously use the computer on a time-sharing system, assuming that the demands of any single user will not be particularly large. Finally, if time delays of an hour or two (unfortunately, sometimes more) are not intolerable, a batch computer system is perfectly acceptable. These options will be investigated in greater depth in the next chapter.

8

OF WHAT USE
ARE DIFFERENT KINDS
OF COMPUTERS?

If you feel that you have some problems that computers could help you to solve, your immediate impulse may be to rush out and buy yourself a computer. If you try to do so, you will discover why most people don't own their own computers —they are very expensive. The cheapest, and least capable, computers cost thousands of dollars, and the most expensive computers may cost several million dollars. Most people share the common plight of not being able to buy their own computer, but they have found a solution—use someone else's. A large industry has grown up based on just this premise. Someone buys a computer at great expense, and then sells the use of this computer, in small pieces, to buyers who cannot afford to have their own machine. The original purchaser makes a profit because he charges more for the use of the computer than he needs to in order to regain his original capital investment and pay for his upkeep and maintenance. Individual users benefit from this arrangement because they are able to get their problems solved at a reasonable cost.

There are many computers available for part-time use by individuals, and they differ in a number of ways. Clearly, one wishes to use a computer that is adequate for the job at hand. On the other hand, it would be a waste to buy computer time on a computer that is more powerful than one needs.

Since there are so many types of machines available, it would be impossible to survey the limitations and strong points of all of the computers that can be used. Rather, in this chapter we will examine the three most popular computer configurations and try to match these configurations with common problems in order to see how well each configuration does with each type of problem.

The computer systems that will be described differ along a number of dimensions, and it is worthwhile to begin by considering these dimensions and to see what they mean. Each computer system has its own unique central processing unit, and associated with this it has a unique word length and instruction set. Central processors differ from each other in a number of ways. One obvious way is speed: clearly, some CPUs are faster than others, and will execute programs at a higher rate. This means that you will need less computer time and might therefore expect to save some money. Unfortunately, faster CPUs tend to be more expensive, and thus more expensive to rent.

Speed of program execution is intimately related to word length. Those machines that have more bits per word seem to execute programs at a higher speed. We find that computers with word lengths of thirty-two bits, thirty-six bits, or sixty bits tend to be faster than those with a smaller number of bits in their words.

Obviously, the instruction sets of different CPUs will differ. Central processors with powerful instruction sets are generally faster than those with more primitive instruction sets. (This need not be true, but it does seem to be a useful rule of thumb.) The main advantage of a more powerful instruction set is the convenience of programming. You can write longer programs and have them working sooner if the instruction set of the computer is congenial. It might appear that the instruction set and word length would be irrelevant if one limited one's programming to languages and compilers such as FORTRAN. Actually, this is not so. Machines with powerful instruction sets and long word lengths usually have more efficient compilers.

Computer systems differ in the amount of memory available: small systems may have as little as one thousand words of memory, and large systems as many as a million words. It is not necessary for a computer to have more memory than you require for your program and for the data that you wish to evaluate, but even one word less than you need may be fatal. Most large-scale computer systems have more memory than you need for most problems. Fortunately, you usually have to pay only for the amount of memory that you use, even though the entire memory is available during the time that your program is being executed.

The most critical differences between computer systems are the peripherals that they have. Many computer systems, for example, have no graphic displays, A-to-D converters, or D-to-A converters. Others have no printer, no magnetic tapes, or no disc. For certain problems, appropriate peripherals are indispensible. If you need an A-to-D converter, nothing else can substitute. On the other hand, certain substitutions can occasionally be made—for example, magnetic tape may be almost as good as a disc for some purposes, and a Teletype can be a replacement, although a frustrating one, for a high-speed printer.

Computers also differ in their operating systems. We have identified three main types of operating systems: interactive operating systems for a single user, time-sharing systems for many users, and batch operating systems for many users. There are, of course, many other varieties but we will not be concerned about them in this book. These operating systems are programs supplied, in general, by the manufacturer of a particular computer. It is not at all uncommon for the manufacturer of a computer to supply all three operating systems when he delivers his machine, and perhaps several more. It is up to the purchaser of the machine to decide which operating system he wishes to run, and whether he wishes to switch among them. For example, it might be reasonable to run a time-sharing operating system between 9:00 and 5:00 and to substitute a batch operating system in the evening hours. The owners of most computers are surprisingly inflexible in their decisions. Generally, they opt to run a single operating system and are loath to make any changes. In those rare cases when they are willing to make changes, the hours of change are usually remarkably inconvenient. Therefore, it pays to look for a computer that is running an operating system of the type that you need for the problems that you wish to solve.

The previous chapters of this book have implied that you deal with computers by physically going to them and interacting with them on a relatively personal basis. In many cases, this is not true. For example, owners of computers that run batch operating systems usually refuse to allow the individual users to touch their machines, or even to come close to them. They usually interpose a computer operator between the user and the computer. The computer operator's job is to receive a deck of cards, containing commands, data, and the like, from the user, carry this deck to the computer (a few feet away), and have the cards read by the computer via a card reader. Such an arrangement satisfies the owner's demand for safety and security.

With time-sharing systems, the personal approach might produce a small traffic problem. Consider forty or fifty people converging on an individual computer, all hoping to use it at once, conveniently, and independently. Although forty or fifty Teletypes may be available, they must be a sufficient distance from each other to afford each user some privacy. One way this could be accomplished would be to have very long wires connecting the Teletype, or other terminal, to the computer. In fact, they may be so long that the terminal would be one or two buildings away from the computer. The use of wires connecting the Teletype to the computer is a burden, and other means of connection have been found: the most common is the telephone system. We know from everyday experience that we can transmit numbers over the telephone. We do so whenever we dial a number and whenever we touch the individual buttons of a touch-tone phone. In the latter case, numbers are transmitted via specially coded tones. Is there any reason why the same, or similar, tones, couldn't be used to transmit numbers between a computer in one location and a peripheral—a terminal—in another location? Both the computer and the terminal could be physically the same as the simple computer-Teletype combination we have been discussing. The only addition is that at each end it would be necessary to produce tones that could be sent over telephone lines and to receive tones from the telephone and convert them into numbers. Such devices are available and are called *acoustic couplers*. This method allows us to use a computer wherever a telephone is available. For example, it is just as easy, using a telephone line, to use a computer 3,000 miles away as it is to use one down the block. It is, however, somewhat more expensive.

There is an important limitation on data transmission via common telephone lines that goes above and beyond the cost factor: the speed with which numbers can be transmitted along a common telephone line is limited. Let's consider the number of bits that can be transmitted from place to place with reasonable accuracy. In most cases, we are currently limited to transmitting about 9,600 bits per second; this is entirely adequate if we are only concerned with typing information into the computer. If we type at a rate of 10 characters per second (and this is a very fast rate), we need to transmit only about 100 bits per second. However, we should also be concerned about receiving information from the computer at our Teletype printer. In principle, the computer could supply us with information at a high rate, but the telephone lines could not handle that high rate. To this end, high-speed telephone lines are available, and it is possible to transmit data at rates up to millions of bits per second. Such service, however, is not available to the casual user.

We brought up the question of accuracy of data transmission, and it is a serious problem. We have all had the experience of hearing "noise" on our telephone lines when we are speaking, perhaps picking up someone else's conversation, hearing strange "beeps," and the like. For conversational purposes, such noise is annoying, but irrelevant. For data transmission, it may be disastrous. Transmission error rate is generally pretty low, but it depends on the part of the country through which the data is being transmitted, for telephone service is not uniformly excellent everywhere we live. In some places, for example, the accuracy of transmission is so low that communicating with a computer via telephone lines may be an extraordinarily frustrating experience.

Not all computer systems allow remote access. Furthermore, some problems are well-suited to remote access and others are not. The critical question is whether or not a large amount of data has to be transmitted with high accuracy.

Keeping the differences between computers in mind, we can begin to explore the three most common computer systems in use. The first is the *dedicated mini-computer*. The name "mini-computer" gives away some of its characteristics—it is small, in a number of ways. The word length of a mini-computer is less than twenty-four bits; it is frequently sixteen bits or twelve bits. The mini-computer's CPU is usually inexpensive, and it has an unsophisticated instruction set. Recently, mini-computers have been developed with quite sophisticated and interesting instruction sets, but they are in the minority. The mini-computer's CPU is among the fastest currently available, if we take into account its short word length. Traditionally, mini-computer systems have very little memory (4,000 to 16,000 words) and few peripherals. Peripherals might include a small disc, a Teletype, and perhaps an A-to-D converter. There is no good reason why mini-computers cannot have more peripherals, but generally they do not.

Since mini-computers are the cheapest of the three kinds of computer systems to be discussed, they are usually "dedicated." This means, for our purposes, two things. First, mini-computers are often dedicated to a particular kind of problem or task. For example, a single mini-computer may be used exclusively for computerized typesetting at a newspaper, control of experiments in a laboratory, production of graphic displays for movie-making, or the like. Frequently, mini-computers are dedicated in that they are used by a single user at a time. This is not to say that mini-computers cannot run time-sharing operating systems or batch operating systems—they can and often do. Nevertheless, in most cases the operating systems that are run by mini-computers are for a single interactive user. The interaction may be considered as a cycle. First, the user uses the editor to prepare a program, then he uses the assembler and loader to run the program, after which he repeats the cycle, modifying the original program or creating a new one. During the running of his program, the entire power of the computer is available to him.

The second type of computer is the *time-sharing system*. Time-sharing systems are usually based on large, fast computers that can handle the requirements of several users apparently simultaneously. Often these users are remote from the computer and interact with it via telephone lines. The central processing unit of time-sharing systems is usually quite fast, and has a sophisticated instruction set and a long word length. Specialized electrical hardware may be attached to the central processor in order to assist it in handling the simultaneous requests of a number of computer users. Peripherals for a time-sharing system often include large discs, magnetic tapes, high speed printers, and high speed card readers. The reason for the use of the large discs and magnetic tape is obvious—with several users, there is a large quantity of numbers that have to be stored. The requirement of a high speed card reader and a high speed printer is also fairly important: if either device were slow, a long line of waiting users might result.

Payment is made by the user of a time-sharing system on a number of bases. You pay for the number of hours you are "connected" to the computer via the telephone lines, the number of seconds the central processor has to devote toward handling your requests for service, the amount of memory that you require to run your programs, the amount of disc space and magnetic tape storage space that you require to store your programs and data, the number of cards that you read into the computer, and the number of lines that are printed as output on the high speed printer. Despite the number of charges, the expenses of using a time-sharing system are usually quite small, especially for the common moderate problems for which it was originally designed. With the mini-computer you must pay for and receive the services of the entire computer for the time that you want it. With a time-sharing system you pay for only part of the computer (because there are also many other users), and yet you receive the services of what appears to be a complete computer, although it may be a slow and irregular one. If speed and regularity are not critical, time-sharing systems may be the solution to your problem. They are certainly one of the most convenient computer systems to use, for you may locate your Teletype terminal in your home, office, or anywhere you like, completely independent of the location of the computer. At any time of the day or night you can dial the computer on a common telephone via a special telephone number and be at work within minutes. This description assumes, of course, that the telephones are working properly, that the time-sharing computer is not broken, and that the computer is not currently being used by as many users as it can handle, in which case it will simply not answer your call.

The typical batch computer is physically similar to the time-sharing system described, except that it does not have fifty or sixty Teletypes connected as peripherals. The batch computer is inconvenient to use in that you have to bring your problem to the computer; you don't have a terminal of the computer conveniently located for your use. It is possible, of course, to have a card reader and high speed printer located remotely from the main batch computer—in your home, for example. The only limitation to this utopia is the cost, which is prohibitively high. In addition, the owner of a batch computer may be reluctant to allow you such a facility unless you guarantee to use the computer a minimum number of hours per month—a minimum number that may be quite high.

As noted in the last chapter, batch operating systems can receive commands for service at almost any time from a number of users. They fulfill requests for service more or less in the order in which they are received. The qualifier "more or less" is included because the operator of a batch system almost always has the option of reordering the requests that are being stored by the computer. Hopefully, he will make such reorderings to improve efficiency. When you submit a series of requests to the batch computer, you may be at the end of a long line of such requests, and it may be several hours, or more, before your task is completed. This turn-around time is the bane of the existence of batch computer system users. In some cases long waits for computer returns are unimportant, but in others they are intolerable. One reason for using a batch operating system rather than a time-sharing system is that for a given problem it is probably somewhat less expensive to use a batch system. It is an individual decision as to whether the money saved is worth the delays involved.

I have selected several problems that are examples of those most commonly encountered. Your own problems may not fit exactly into any of the classes presented, but hopefully some of them will come close. For each example, I will try to discuss the reasons why the problem is better suited for one type of computer than for another, if, in fact, a proper match exists.

The first example is a problem for which a lot of information has to be read into the computer, a short and simple computer program must be run using all of that information, and then a lot of information must be created by the computer. This problem may be termed a high input-output and low computation problem. A typical example might be a common business payroll. Because of the large amount of information that must go into and come out of the computer, appropriate peripherals must be available. Furthermore, they should be of reasonably high speed. This requirement almost eliminates the use of remote peripherals—communicating with a computer via telephone lines. The exception would be if special telephone lines were used so that high speeds of data transmission could be accomplished. Because the computation performed is essentially trivial, it is not necessary to have a very powerful central processing unit, that is, one with a long word length, sophisticated instruction set, or high speed of instruction execution. However, since a large amount of data is involved, a good deal of memory is required. Problems of this sort are usually done on batch machines. Batch machines provide a low cost for the computation, a large memory, and high speed peripherals for input and output of information. Such computations could be performed on an appropriate mini-computer system, but mini-computers with large memories and high speed peripherals are not commonly encountered. A time-sharing system is the least suitable for this sort of problem, for a number of reasons. For one thing, interaction is usually either unnecessary or impossible with a job of this sort. For another, the remote access necessitated by most time-sharing systems decreases the speed of data transmission to a point where an individual job might take many hours.

The antithesis of the problem just presented is one in which there is very little input, very little output, and a lot of computation. Physicists commonly have this sort of problem. A time-sharing solution is perfectly acceptable from the point of view of input and output, but may not be acceptable because of the low speed of program execution. If the program to be executed requires only a minute or two of time-sharing computer time, perhaps such a solution is reasonable. However, these problems can frequently mount up to hours of computer time, and the time-sharing solution is unfeasible. The mini-computer solution is also impractical, but for a different reason. Since the word length of mini-computers is short and the instruction sets of most mini-computers are unsophisticated, the time necessary to execute a complicated calculation would be prohibitively long. We again return to the batch computer, where jobs are run individually, the central processing unit is fast, has a long word length, and has a sophisticated instruction set. Although turn-around time may be an onerous burden, the batch computer may be the only system financially practical for problems of this sort.

Some problems are hard to solve: the computer programs required to solve them might require a small or moderate amount of input or output and short or moderate length programs. With a difficult problem, each program you run could lead you to immediately want to run another, different program. This may be because the previous program was wrong in some small way, or because its results suggested another attack on the problem at hand. Here you would need an interactive system, and time-sharing systems come into their own. Because of the small input and output demands and the short run times of the individual programs, the numerous users of a time-sharing system and the associated low speed are not a problem. The magnificent advantage of the time-sharing system for problems of this sort is the continuous interaction between the user and the computer. You can create and run programs at a dizzying speed and feel as if you are getting closer and closer to the solution of your problem. Under such circumstances, the interaction between the user and the computer appears to be rather rapid. Actually, each waits for the other. Such waits are not necessarily a burden. For example, you may not mind waiting one or two seconds for the time-sharing computer to complete a request that you have made. Similarly, while you are typing your request the computer can attend to the request of another user.

Unfortunately, computers sometimes have to interact with processes that are more impatient than the human users of time-sharing systems. For example, consider the problem of controlling traffic in a major city, regulating the processes in a chemical production plant, or measuring the electrocardiagram of a patient in a hospital. In all of these examples, the computer must interact with a real-world process that goes on at its own rate. The electrocardiogram does not slow down for the computer—the computer must keep up with the electrocardiogram. Similarly, the liquids in a chemical plant will spill at the rate that the laws of physics demand, regardless of the speed or efficiency of the computer attempting to control the process. Problems of this sort may be termed *real-time problems*. To solve a real-time problem, the computer must be able to keep up with external events. Computers could not be used to assist in air traffic control at major airports if their performance were erratic. A delay of a second or two might be critical for the safety of a number of planes and their passengers.

Time-sharing systems are unsuitable for many real-time processes. If a time-sharing system is attempting to control two real-time processes at once, it would not be unreasonable or unusual for both to require service at almost the same time. With some real-time processes, it may be intolerable if one has to wait. Therefore, we must use a dedicated computer.

In principle, any dedicated computer would do the job, as long as it was fast enough. In practice, small dedicated computers, mini-computers, are most commonly used. The obvious reason for this is cost. As you will remember, the deficiencies of the typical mini-computer system are a small memory, few peripherals, and relatively unsophisticated instruction sets. What should we do with real-time problems that require, in addition to fast response, occasional complicated calculation and large storage capabilities for data? One solution that has been adopted with some success is to connect a mini-computer to a larger computer, such as a time-sharing system or a batch system. The mini-computer would control the process at hand on a second-to-second (or microsecond-to-microsecond) basis. When necessary, however, the larger computer would store masses of data transmitted to it from the mini-computer, or perform complex calculations. Shipments of data from mini-computer to large computer, or for that matter, from one computer to any other, are not necessarily more complicated than shipments of data between a central processing unit and a peripheral. Numbers can be transmitted over wires (a *bus*), or, if time allows, over the telephone lines.

EPILOGUE

At this point you should be able to determine whether or not your problems can be solved through the use of computers and you should be able to choose the computer system best suited for your needs. Obtain a manual for the computer you are interested in, read it, learn the instruction set, and write programs for it. Probably none of your programs will work the first time, or even the second time, but if you persevere, eventually they will work. There is no doubt that you will make mistakes. You will probably continue to make mistakes for some time, but with decreasing frequency.

APPENDIX A

BINARY AND
OCTAL ARITHMETIC

When we write a number, say 27, we are using a complex symbol to represent a specific magnitude. Our usual number system allows us to represent any magnitude with an arbitrary degree of precision. No magnitude is too large or too small to be accurately represented. Furthermore, our representation for each magnitude is unique. That is, there is only one way to write a particular numerical value.

We can easily conceive of other representations that might be used for magnitudes. For example, we might have a special symbol to represent every possible magnitude. In this case, it would be necessary for us to memorize and accurately manipulate an infinite number of special symbols. Such a system would be unwieldy.

A first step toward simplification would be to limit the symbols in a number system to a small group and to represent a variety of magnitudes with combinations of these basic symbols. For example, the basic symbols that we use are the ten digits, 0, 1, 2, 3, 4, 5, 6, 7, 8, and 9. The way that we usually combine basic symbols into more complex symbols representing a magnitude is not the only way that it can be done. The complex symbol representing a magnitude might consist of a string of digits such that the sum of the values in the string is equal to the particular magnitude. To take a specific example, the magnitude that we usually write as "27" might be alternatively written as "999" or "8883" or "8388" or many other ways. The important point is that there can be a number of representations for any magnitude, and with this approach the order of the digits doesn't make any difference. This system, too, is unacceptable. For a large number, the complexity of the symbol we use to represent its magnitude would be too great —the symbol would be many digits long. Because of the lack of uniqueness, it would not be immediately apparent whether two numbers were the same or different (for example, is 999 the same magnitude as 8883?).

Our number system is based on a finite set of simple symbols, ten digits, which combine to form more complex numbers. The way in which they are combined is important. They are written next to each other, in "places," and each "place" has a value. You will recognize the concept of "place" from elementary school arithmetic. There is a "ones place," a "tens place," a "hundreds place," and so on. The digit in each place represents the number of ones, the number of tens, the number of hundreds and so on. Thus, the number 503 represents a magnitude consisting of 5 hundreds, 0 tens, and 3 ones.

We may inquire why there are ten basic digits in our number system. What would happen if one were missing or another were added? Well, consider the situation if the digit "9" were missing. It would be impossible to represent many magnitudes, such as 9, 90, 49, or any other magnitude currently represented by a number containing the digit "9." Our system would be unacceptable because it could not represent all possible magnitudes. What if an additional digit were added representing some magnitude, say "X" for the magnitude "10." In that case, we could represent the magnitude 10 in two ways—"10" or the special symbol "X." Using this new symbol, the number "XX" would have a magnitude of 10 tens and 10 ones, equivalent to the more usual representation "110." Thus, we would no longer have uniqueness—numbers could be represented more than one way. Having ten digits, 0 through 9, is just right.

In our ordinary system, the values of the individual places in a number are based on the number "10." That is, the magnitude represented by each place is 10, 10 times 10, 10 times 10 times 10, and so on. The only exception is the ones place. Is there anything magical about the number "10"? Could we also have a numerical representation similar to our own based on another number, say "8"? Our common number system is called the "base 10 system." Could there be a "base 8 system"?

A base 8 numerical representation system, or octal system, can be constructed similar to the base 10 system. We will have a ones place, an eights place, a sixty-fours place, a five-hundred-and-twelves place, and so on. Digits in each place of a number would represent a number of ones, a number of eights, a number of sixty-fours, a number of five-hundred-and-twelves and so on, just as digits in particular places represent a number of ones, a number of tens, a number of hundreds, or a number of thousands in a base 10 representation.

If we write the number "237" and claim that it is written "octally," what magnitude does this represent? That is, what is the equivalent base 10 number? We can easily calculate this by adding 2 sixty-fours, 3 eights, and 7 ones, to get a total of 159. Why is it that the base 10 representation of the magnitude looks so much smaller than the base 8 representation? This is really not surprising, since each place in the base 8 representation represents a smaller magnitude—8 versus 10, 64 versus 100, 512 versus 1,000, and so on. It is not surprising that you need "more" in each place in order to make up the same magnitude.

Do we still use the same digits, 0 through 9, in our base 8 system? If so, consider the magnitude we usually write as "8." In our new system, one way of accomplishing this would be to simply write "8," as before, which indicates 8 ones. Another way would be to write "10," indicating 1 eight and 0 ones. Consider the number we commonly write as "9." In the octal system it could be written "9" or it could be written "11," indicating 1 eight and 1 one. There is some ambiguity—some numbers can be written more than one way. For this reason, it is useful to restrict the digits in an octal representation to those between 0 and 7. Using 0, 1, 2, 3, 4, 5, 6, and 7, we can write any number and can do so uniquely. If we restrict the basic set of digits any further, there will be some numbers that we can't write. This is exactly parallel to our previous discussion with base 10, where we saw that the deletion of a digit (in that case, "9") reduced the numbers we could represent, and the addition of a digit (in that case, "X," representing magnitude "10") provided ambiguous representations for magnitude.

What is a binary representation for numbers? It is a number system based on 2; individual places within a number have magnitudes of ones, twos, fours, eights, sixteens, thirty-twos, sixty-fours and so on. Thus, the number "10" in the base 2 or binary system represents a magnitude of 1 two and 0 ones. Numbers written base 2 look even larger than those written base 8. Again, this is because the values represented by each place are considerably less than those in base 8. What digits can be used in a base 2 system? Clearly, 0 and 1 are necessary: if we have more digits, however, such as 2, 3, etc., we find that we can represent individual numbers in several ways. For example, the magnitude "3" might be represented with a single digit "3" meaning 3 ones, or it could be represented "11" meaning 1 two and 1 one. This ambiguity should be avoided, so the digits used in a binary number system are restricted to "0" and "1." What is the base 10 equivalent of the binary number "101101001"? We calculate 1 two-hundred-and-fifty-six, 0 one-hundred-and-twenty-eights, 1 sixty-four, 1 thirty-two, 0 sixteens, 1 eight, 0 fours, 0 twos, and 1 one; a total in base 10 of 361.

There are general rules for converting from one base representation to another base representation, but we will not go into them here. You have seen how to convert from base 8 to base 10, and from base 2 to base 10. Therefore, if you ever see an octal or binary number you should be able to convert it to a magnitude that you can more readily understand.

The individual symbols within a base 10 representation of a number are called *digits*. The individual symbols within a base 2 representation of a number are called *bits*—a bit is comparable to a digit in a base 10 number. Thus, the binary number 1011 is four bits long. It is equivalent in magnitude to 1 eight, 0 fours, 1 two and 1 one, or the magnitude of 11 in base 10. The individual symbols within an octal number have no commonly accepted name.

APPENDIX B

REFERENCES

Bell, C. Gordon, and Allen Newell, *Computer Structures: Readings and Examples.* New York: McGraw-Hill Book Company, 1971. This is a great book about the variety of computer architectures that have been developed. It proposes an interesting method of description for both computer architecture and instruction sets.

Knuth, Donald E., *The Art of Computer Programming*: Vol. 1, *Fundamental Algorithms*; Vol. 2, *Seminumerical Algorithms*; (more to come). Reading, Mass.: Addison-Wesley Publishing Company, Inc., 1968. These volumes are authoritative and entertaining. The first volume includes an excellent discussion of how information can be organized in the memory of computers. The second volume is concerned with how computers can be used in high-precision arithmetic calculations and how computers can generate random numbers.

Minsky, Marvin L., *Computation: Finite and Infinite Machines.* Englewood Cliffs, N.J.: Prentice-Hall, Inc., 1967. This elementary and readable book is concerned with some theories about the mathematical bases of computers.

Sammet, Jean E. *Programming Languages: History and Fundamentals.* Englewood Cliffs, N.J.: Prentice-Hall, Inc., 1969. This book collects information about a large number of programming languages. It is both encyclopedic and readable.

Selfridge, Oliver G. *A Primer for Fortran IV On-Line.* Cambridge, Mass.: M.I.T. Press, 1972. This book provides a painless way to gain a quick working knowledge of FORTRAN.

APPENDIX C

GLOSSARY

Accumulator. An accumulator is a register sometimes found in the CPU of a computer. The instructions of a computer with an accumulator may read or modify the contents of the accumulator.

Acoustic coupler. A computer peripheral need not be located close to the main computer. It can communicate with the main communicator by transferring numbers back and forth over telephone lines. For transmission over telephone lines, numbers are specially coded as a series of tones. An acoustic coupler transforms numbers into a series of tones, or transforms a series of tones into numbers.

Address. Each word of a computer memory is uniquely identified by a number, called an address. Instructions can read or modify the contents of a word by specifying the address of the word and the operation to be performed on its contents.

Analog-to-digital converter. An analog-to-digital converter changes the magnitude of voltages into numbers that can be read by a computer.

Assembler. An assembler is a computer program that transforms a list of computer instructions, specified by mnemonic descriptions of the instructions, into a list of numbers corresponding to those in-structions. This list of numbers can be interpreted by the CPU of a computer during the execution of a program.

Batch operating system. A batch operating system is a computer program that receives commands from various users to run specific programs. Commands are typically read from a card reader or mag-netic tape. The programs to be run are usually stored on discs, magnetic tape, or punched cards. A batch operating system will either run the programs requested by users in the order in which the requests are made, or will schedule the running of the requested programs in an order that maximally utilizes the resources of the computer.

Bit. A bit is a single place in a binary number, comparable to a single digit in a decimal number.

Bus. A bus is a collection of wires connecting two or more major elements of a computer system, such as peripherals, memory, or a CPU. Numbers are transmitted from one device to another along the bus.

Bus controller. A bus controller is a piece of hardware connected to a bus. It controls the transmission of numbers along the bus from one device to another. It does not allow two or more devices to use the bus at the same time, thus confusing each other's messages.

Byte. A byte is usually part of a binary number that is 8 bits in length. For example, a 16-bit binary number contains two 8-bit bytes.

Cache system. Some computer systems contain several memories differing in speed. For example, a system might contain a slow mem-ory, which requires about a microsecond to access a number in a location, as well as a fast memory, which requires only about 100 nanoseconds to access a number in a location. Computers using a cache system of memory organization have at least one "fast" mem-ory. The CPU always receives its instructions from this fast memory. If an instruction to be executed is in the slow memory, it is trans-ferred to the fast memory before being fetched by the CPU and executed. In this way, the memory with which the CPU interacts is matched in speed to the speed of execution of instructions by the CPU.

Cathode ray tube. The cathode ray tube, or CRT, is a vacuum tube very much like a television picture tube. Pictures can be drawn on the face of the tube under the control of the computer.

Central processing unit. The central processing unit, or CPU, is the part of a computer system that fetches instructions, in numerical form, from the memory of a computer and executes those instruc-tions, thus controlling peripheral devices or modifying memory locations.

Compiler. A compiler is a computer program that translates a description of a procedure for the computer to follow into a list of instructions, in numerical form, that can be executed by the CPU. The description of the procedure is in a form that is reasonably understandable to the user. For example, algebraic problems might be solved by a compiler that translates descriptions consisting of algebraic instructions.

Digital-to-analog converter. A digital-to-analog converter changes numbers that can be read by a computer into magnitudes of voltages.

Direct addressing. Most computer instructions contain two types of information: one is the kind of operation to be performed, and the other is the location of the number or numbers in memory to be accessed. One way that the location of the number or numbers to be accessed can be described is by including their address in the instruction. This is known as direct addressing.

Directory. A directory is a list of numbers, usually on a disc or on magnetic tape, that code information regarding the contents of the rest of the disc or magnetic tape. Assuming that the information on the disc or magnetic tape consists of several lists of numbers, the directory contains information about the location of each list of numbers, and some identifying information about each list.

Disc. A disc is a computer peripheral used for storing numbers. It consists of a metal disc, magnetized on one or both sides. Binary numbers are stored on the disc by magnetizing or demagnetizing individual points on the disc surface.

Editor. An editor is a computer program that transfers characters from a computer peripheral controlled by a user to another device in a computer system. For example, an editor might transfer characters typed by a user on a teletype to paper tape, a disc, or magnetic tape. In addition, an editor gives a user the facility to correct mistakes that he has made while inputting characters.

FORTRAN. FORTRAN is a set of rules for describing arithmetic problems to be solved by a computer. A problem, properly described using the rules of FORTRAN, can be transformed, by a FORTRAN compiler, to a list of numbers that form instructions to be executed by the CPU for solving the arithmetic problem.

Indirect addressing. A computer instruction usually contains information about an operation to be performed. It also contains information about the location in memory of the number or numbers to be modified by that operation. The location of the number (or numbers) to be modified may be coded by placing, in an instruction, an address that contains the address of the location in memory to be modified. This coding scheme is called indirect addressing.

Immediate addressing. Computer instructions that use a number during their execution (for example, an instruction to multiply by 10) may have that number included in the instruction. In that case, the number is said to be immediately addressed.

Instruction. An instruction is a number that can be stored in a computer memory. Instructions are taken from the computer memory by the central processor, and are interpreted by the central processor. Thus, each instruction causes the central processing unit to do one particular thing.

Instruction set. The instruction set for a computer is a set of numbers, each of which is an instruction. All instructions for a computer are included within a description of its instruction set. Note that all numbers are not instructions and hence all numbers are not included in the instruction set for any particular computer.

Loader. A loader is a computer program that transfers a program stored on a disc, magnetic tape, paper tape, or the like, to the memory of a computer. More powerful loaders may be able to transfer several programs to computer memory, start programs, or combine many small programs into a single large program.

Memory. The memory of a computer is an electronic device that stores numbers. Each number is limited in size (it cannot be too large or too small) and is in a specific location or word of the memory. Individual locations or words in memory are uniquely identified by a number—their address.

Mini-computer. A mini-computer is usually a computer with a relatively short word length. Common word lengths include 8 bits, 12 bits, 16 bits, and 18 bits.

Multiport memory. A multiport memory is a memory that can be connected to two or more CPUs. The CPUs can independently access words in memory, and each can access words in memory at approximately the full speed of the memory.

Multi-programming. Multi-programming is a technique used by some batch operating systems. Several programs are kept in memory at one time, in whole or in part, and the CPU switches among them in order to maximize usage of the computer facilities.

Op code. Each computer instruction contains information about an operation to be performed and the location of numbers on which the operation is to be performed. That part of the instruction telling what operation is to be performed is the op code.

Operating system. An operating system is a computer program dedicated to helping users make more efficient use of their computer facilities. An operating system may consist of a loader, assembler, compilers, editors, and other helpful programs. In addition, it allows the user easy access to these programs and to his own program.

Peripheral. A peripheral is a device in a computer system that allows the computer to store numbers or interact with the outside world. Peripherals for storing numbers include discs and magnetic tape. Peripherals for input/output include graphic displays, paper tape readers, card readers, printers, etc.

Plotter. A plotter is a computer peripheral used for drawing line pictures on paper.

Program. A computer program is a list of instructions, frequently in numerical form, that are sequentially executed by a CPU.

Program counter. A program counter is a register in the CPU that always contains the address of the next instruction to be executed. It may be modified automatically by the CPU, by an instruction, or by switches on the front of the computer.

Register. A register is a very small memory. It consists of only one word, hence it can store only one number at a single address.

Relative addressing. The location of a number or numbers in memory to be accessed by an instruction may be coded in that instruction by specifying the address of the number or numbers relative to the locations of the instruction. This is known as relative addressing.

Storage tube. A storage tube is a cathode ray tube that stores a picture drawn on its face almost indefinitely. The entire picture can be erased under computer control.

Subroutine. A subroutine is a program used repetitively by a main program to perform a fixed task.

Tablet. A tablet is a peripheral that allows one to draw a picture and transfer a description of that picture to a computer.

Time-sharing system. A computer system that is a time-sharing system uses a special operating system for time-sharing. This allows several users to use the computer almost simultaneously and be unaware of each other's presence.

Vector generator. A vector generator is a computer peripheral for drawing straight lines on a CRT. The computer controls the drawing by giving the vector generator the locations of the end points of the line to be drawn.

Word. A word is a single location in memory at which a number may be stored.

Word length. The word length of a computer is the maximum number of bits that can be contained in any binary number stored in words of its memory.

INDEX

5466